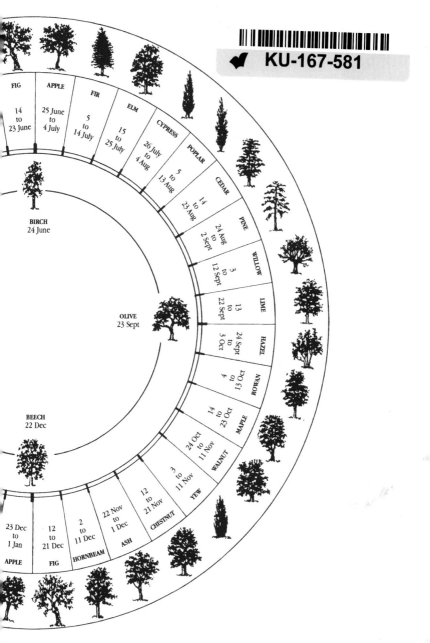

FIG
14
to
23 June

APPLE
25 June
to
4 July

FIR
5
to
14 July

ELM
15
to
25 July

CYPRESS
26 July
to
4 Aug

POPLAR
5
to
13 Aug

CEDAR
14
to
23 Aug

PINE
24 Aug
to
2 Sept

WILLOW
3
to
12 Sept

LIME
13
to
22 Sept

HAZEL
24 Sept
to
3 Oct

ROWAN
4
to
13 Oct

MAPLE
14
to
23 Oct

WALNUT
24 Oct
to
11 Nov

YEW
3
to
11 Nov

CHESTNUT
12
to
21 Nov

ASH
22 Nov
to
1 Dec

HORNBEAM
2
to
11 Dec

FIG
12
to
21 Dec

APPLE
23 Dec
to
1 Jan

BIRCH
24 June

OLIVE
23 Sept

BEECH
22 Dec

THE CELTIC
TREE CALENDAR

THE CELTIC TREE CALENDAR

YOUR TREE SIGN AND YOU

MICHAEL VESCOLI

Translated from the German by Rosemary Dear

Illustrated by Jean-Claude Senée

SOUVENIR PRESS

This book is a translation of *Der Keltischer Baumkalender*,
a revised edition of the book originally published in 1988 by
Edition M, Zürich under the title *Keltische Baumkreis*,
first published in 1995 by Heinrich Hugendubel Verlag, München
© Heinrich Hugendubel Verlag, München

English translation Copyright © 1999
by Souvenir Press and Rosemary Dear
Illustrations by Jean-Claude Senée
Copyright © Actes Sud, 1996

First English edition published 1999 by
Souvenir Press Ltd.,
43 Great Russell Street, London WC1B 3PA

ISBN 0 285 63463 1

Typeset by Rowland Phototypesetting Limited,
Bury St Edmunds, Suffolk
Printed and bound in Singapore

CONTENTS

The World of the Celts   9

   The Celts   10

   The Druids   19

   The Celtic Tree Calendar   22

The oak: symbol of the life force   30

The hazel: the tree that wants to be first   36

The rowan: the favourite of the birds   41

The maple: a quarrelsome angel?   47

The walnut: searching for its homeland   52

The poplar: the tree that overcomes uncertainty   57

The chestnut: in quest of its truth   63

The ash: aspiring to the heights   68

The hornbeam: a monument to loyalty   74

The fig: a very accommodating tree   80

The birch: the tree of initiation   85

The beech: the one who waits   91

The apple: fulfilment in love   96

The fir: guardian of all births   101

The elm: the good-tempered tree   107
The cypress: the tree of resurrection   116
The cedar: the tree of nobility   122
The pine: mother of wisdom   127
The willow: a many-sided citizen of the world   133
The lime: the nurse of the oak   139
The olive: the tree that lives wisely   145
The yew: the outcast tree of death   151

Further reading   159

THE CELTIC TREE CALENDAR

	Oak 21 Mar		**Olive** 23 Sept
22–31 Mar		Hazel	24 Sept–3 Oct
1–10 April		Rowan	4–13 Oct
11–20 April		Maple	14–23 Oct
21–30 April		Walnut	24 Oct–11 Nov
1–14 May		**Poplar**	
15–24 May		Chestnut	12–21 Nov
25 May–3 June		Ash	22 Nov–1 Dec
4–13 June		Hornbeam	2–11 Dec
14–23 June		Fig	12–21 Dec

	Birch 24 June		**Beech** 22 Dec
25 June–4 July		Apple	23 Dec–1 Jan
5–14 July		Fir	2–11 Jan
15–25 July		Elm	12–24 Jan
26 July–4 Aug		Cypress	25 Jan–3 Feb
5–13 Aug		**Poplar**	4–8 Feb
14–23 Aug		Cedar	9–18 Feb
24 Aug–2 Sept		Pine	19–29 Feb
3–12 Sept		Willow	1–10 Mar
13–22 Sept		Lime	11–20 Mar

Yew
3–11 Nov

THE WORLD OF THE CELTS

Two to three thousand years ago, when we humans were still living in close proximity with nature, the tree calendar originated as a development of the stone circles which the Celts had discovered when they arrived in Western Europe. As 'conquerors', they probably adopted many of the traditions of the resident population. We do not know. Many conflicting legends have come down from an era which lies shrouded in the mists of time. But we have an inbuilt access to this past, for the complex mosaic of our inner feelings—of fear and joy, strength and weakness, pleasure and sadness, security and despair, and many other emotions—is as strong in us today as it was in the people of those times. Through our feelings we can imagine ourselves in the culture of our forebears, in the magic inner world of the 'childhood of mankind'.

And the Celtic tree calendar is also our

passport to the past, for it is a 'spiritual collage', a combination of information about trees, the ancient division of time and practical knowledge about people, seasoned with the pepper of magic and the salt of spirituality. Originally this book had the title *The Celtic Tree Circle*, to remind us that a perfect circle has been a symbol of the soul since time immemorial. That is why the calendar is shown in the form of a circle, for it is a calendar of a very special kind: it brings to light hidden correlations between the world of trees and the nature of human beings.

THE CELTS

The Celts, called Keltoi by the Greeks and Gauls by the Romans, belonged to the western group of 'Indo-European' peoples. Towards the end of the third millennium before Christ, when the Scythians wandering through the Russian steppes began to spread out, the Celts were forced to advance towards the west and to fan out gradually over all of Europe. In the north they settled in England, Scotland and Ireland. In the west they came across Northern Spain and into Portugal. In the south they settled in the Po Valley, attacked the Etruscans and even captured Rome in 387 BC, after a Roman

ambassador had killed one of their leaders. Yet there
was never a Celtic empire.

It can be claimed that the Celts were incapable
of founding a great nation because they were always
quarrelling amongst themselves and each tribe was
only concerned with its own advantage. Certainly
this contributed a great deal to their decline. But
during their rise to prominence and in their prime
(950–52 BC), their religious and cultural unity and
their linguistic and economic cohesion were such
that they were an empire in all but name. All that

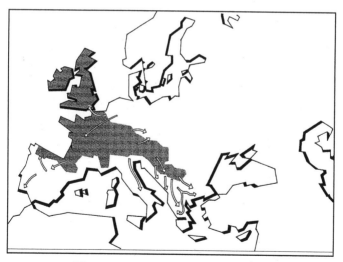

The extent of Celtic expansion in Europe.

was missing was some kind of imperial honour for their most senior druid.

The druids, and through them the Celts, professed belief in another world, in the immortality of the soul and so in reincarnation. The history and the behaviour of the Celts is incomprehensible without taking these basic beliefs into account. These were what made them stubborn, bold and ready for adventure. They filled with terror those who feared death. But after victory and defeat alike they were quickly reconciled with their enemies, intermarried with their subjects and gave loyal support to their new masters, so long as they were treated fairly. They withdrew from the towns and countries they had conquered, not from some whim or other, but because they believed that this world was only a temporary arrangement—their real homeland was waiting for them in the Next World.

People who believe in the immortality of the soul do not need to accumulate power, build empires or prepare lasting defences. It is enough to make provision for the essentials of life and to enjoy living. Deadly seriousness does not fit with the Celtic character. A Celt enjoys everything life has to offer, but he does not sell his immortal soul for it.

Nevertheless it is not the impetuousness of

the Celts who swept through Europe with their swords in their hands that makes them unforgettable. It is the innumerable practical inventions which we find today wherever we turn: the axe, the hammer, the hatchet, scissors, the plumb-line, the hand cart, the horseshoe and whatever else is forged from iron—the Celts refined them all to such a level that they could hardly be improved. They are the great people of the Iron Age. Their hard-working wheelwrights developed the wheeled plough. Their ingenious smelters and smiths not only produced unparalleled weapons, they also invented the scythe, the pitchfork, the shovel and other implements which all farming peoples use.

They are still remembered, too, for their knowledge of nature: for they did not limit their knowledge to the use of the trees that sheltered them, they also studied plants and their effects and knew how to evaluate them and use them correctly as remedies. Their herbal lore lies at the root of modern Western herbalism.

Timetable of Celtic History

1000–800 BC. The Celts begin to play their historic role in Central Europe with the appearance of iron.
900 BC. The Goidelic Celts (ancestors of the Scots

and Irish) migrate to Britain and penetrate as far as Ireland.

800–500 BC. The Celts are at the forefront of what is known as the Hallstatt period. This is characterised by an astonishing wealth of metal objects of all kinds (swords, knives, spear tips, axes). It is well known for its large bronze vessels depicting daily life with its sacrificial ceremonies, combat and magnificent banquets. At that time Hallstatt, an Austrian village in the Salzkammergut, was the richest and most important focal point of the Iron Age. The reason for this wealth was an extensive salt trade.

500 BC. The Brythonic Celts (ancestors of the Welsh) migrate to Britain. Celtic culture is in full flower. This period is called La Tène after the place of that name in Switzerland, near the Neuenburgersee, where many finds were discovered. Their art is basically utilitarian, but at the same time they also like stylised ornamentation: leaf-shaped raised ribbons, bulging eyes, palmettes, snails and many others. The Celts proved themselves masters of more than just the art of iron-working. Their gold, silver and bronze jewellery, sometimes with enamel decoration, points to craftsmanship of a high standard. They were the first north European people to mint coins. They didn't portray human heads, gods, heroes or kings on them, but signs and symbols of their mystic perception of the world.

400 BC. The Insubres tribe destroy the Etruscan town of Melprum and build it again as Mediolanum (Milan). The Semnones divide up Umbria and the Adriatic. Others advance to Apulia and Sicily.

387 BC. The Celts take Rome, but not the Capitol, which is saved by the cackling of geese.

379–368 BC. Dionysus of Syracuse's campaign against the Lokri.

336–323 BC. Celts from several tribes fight on the side of Alexander the Great in his campaign to conquer Greece. During the conquest of the Persian Empire they provide the main force of his army, numbering just 40,000 warriors, which in 334 BC crosses the Hellespont and brings the whole of Asia Minor, Egypt and Greater Persia (Iraq, Iran, Pakistan, Afghanistan, Turkestan, Buchara and parts of India) under the rule of Alexander.

279 BC. Led by Bolgios and Brennos, the Celts invade Greece and threaten Delphi. It is said that Brennos laughed at the Greeks because they portrayed their gods in human form.

277 BC. Antigonos Gonatas beats the Tectosages, the Trocmi and the Tolistoboii in a night battle and is acknowledged King of Macedonia. Nicomedes, who is fighting Antiochus I for the Bithynian part of Asia

Minor, enlists the three Celtic tribes who have just been defeated as reinforcements.

275 BC. Antiochus defeats the Celts in Asia Minor. Nicomedes gives them a region near Ankara to settle in. Galatia is founded. Byzantium suffers attacks by the Tylian Celts.

230 BC. Attalos I beats the Galatii in the valley of the Kaikos and is so impressed by them that he leaves a Gaulish votive offering in the shrine of Pallas Athene at Pergamon.

218 BC. The Second Punic War begins. Hannibal marches with an enormous army through Spain and southern France and over the Alps against Rome. Instead of forming an alliance with him, the neighbouring Celtic tribes make it more difficult for him on the march through. The Celts in upper Italy give him their half-hearted support and he can only rely on the Boii tribe. Hannibal loses the war, and so the Celts have let slip their last chance to stop the expansion of the Roman Empire.

175 BC. End of the Roman campaign against the Celts of Upper Italy.

133 BC. Beginning of the campaigns by the Iberian Celts against Rome.

75 BC. The Belgian Gauls begin to cross the Channel.

61 BC. Julius Caesar breaks the last Celtic resistance in Spain.

58–51 BC. Caesar defeats the Gauls.

55 and 54 BC. Caesar sails to Britain and fights against the Belgians who had migrated there, but they continue to spread out there.

52 and 51 BC. Vercingetorix succeeds in uniting several tribes under his leadership. He hits on the idea of the 'scorched earth' tactic: women and children will have to hide as best they can, and the villages and towns with their provisions must be burnt to the ground so that the Roman legions will be driven away by hunger. One tribe, the Bituriges, refuses to sacrifice its beautiful, rich capital. 'If you think you can defend yourselves you are mistaken', Vercingetorix tells them, 'but if that is what you really want, that's up to you!' From a distance the remnants of the remaining tribes can only watch as the Roman siege warfare machine notches up yet another success. Vercingetorix has difficulty in preventing his warriors from intervening, for, as he predicted, Avaricum cannot be held. Of the 40,000 inhabitants and defenders of the town only 800 survive. Caesar knows that this is just a Pyrrhic victory and withdraws to the south. The Gauls follow him. Vercingetorix only allows them to attack the baggage train on the strict understanding that they will immediately turn back if the Romans form up into their 'square'. In the heat of battle the

Celts forget all precautions and in their only encounter they throw away all the successes so sorely won by guerrilla warfare. Caesar, used to reacting quickly as situations develop, catches them in his famous pincer movement. After the bloody defeat Vercingetorix escapes with his remaining warriors to Alésia, which he holds for only 40 days. He knows that with the fall of Alésia the Celtic cause is lost and allows himself to be taken captive. In 46 BC he is executed in Rome.

50 BC is generally accepted as the end of the La Tène Period. From this time onwards the history of the Celts on the European continent is almost completely eclipsed by that of the Romans. But the heyday of the Celts had really come to an end between 200 and 150 BC. Until approximately 200 BC the druids and Celts had been, as it were, a unified whole. Then the druids, and gradually the Celts as well, fell victim to dissent over their basic perception of the world, which became increasingly difficult to patch up.

This timetable gives just a rough outline and is far from complete, quite apart from the fact that we have only Roman and Greek sources and archaeologists to thank for these dates. The Celts themselves failed to provide any written records of their victories and defeats, or of their heroes, princes and kings. They had a tendency to care as little about the past as they did about speculation on the future. They lived very much for the present, having learnt from their druids that writing weakened the power of the events that had been recorded. Everything worth knowing had to be handed down by word of mouth, varying with each repetition. In order to remember better, they linked these things with other vitally important information which was transmitted in pictures and symbols appealing directly to the feelings.

In my view the Celtic way of learning was the basis of their success. Where the consideration of human feelings remains paramount, the ethical principles of Celtic culture have been preserved down to the present time. Their philosophy of life reached such a level that we can count it unreservedly as an eternal human truth.

THE DRUIDS

In the Celtic language *drui* is the generally accepted term for an 'initiate'. We tend to regard the druids as a 'priest class', but that would give the wrong impression. To the Celts they were especially far-seeing and knowledgeable, people who ventured to go into the depths of the wood and therefore overcame the fear of the darkness of the inner life.

People hungry for knowledge, who were as interested in the community as they were in themselves, became druids. Anyone who felt drawn to art, who liked to make music and sing, entered the community of the druids, as well as those religious seekers who longed for answers to the fundamental questions of being. This community formed the cultural elite of the vast Celtic national community, which embraced at least 60 tribes, if not twice that number, spread out over the whole of Europe as far as Turkey.

This community was rigidly structured, not only within the tribes or within a region, but also in the whole area of the early Celtic community. Each tribe had its 'chief druid'. Regions had 'chief druids', and in the council of 'chief druids' of all the Celts there was one who took on the leadership either on the basis of his importance, his merit or because he had been elected by the other druids. Membership of the druid community was not hereditary, nor were any 'duties', offices or responsibilities. If a druid died, the most capable person took over his 'duties'. If there were several contenders for a 'key position' a vote was taken among the most senior druids. The druid community was therefore neither a caste like, for example, the Brahmin community in India, nor a kind of collegiate body which unilaterally decided what was good for the Celts. Its members directed the fate of their tribes from the background. They were the advisers, the doctors, the seers, the teachers and the entertainers, not just for 'princes' and 'kings', but also for ordinary people.

The druids carried out their duty to those who were in need and helped to deal with problems. For that they were not just revered, but also cared for on a voluntary basis. Their only privilege was exemption from tax liabilities and military service. If they wanted to they could bear arms and go into battle; more frequently they acted as arbitrators in tribal feuds.

According to the Romans the druids placed themselves between opposing armies and sang songs full of mystery until both sides sounded the retreat. It is known that they enjoyed great respect and exercised even greater authority.

At a time when autocrats everywhere still claimed to be appointed by the gods, the druids cleverly and wisely confined themselves to intellectual and spiritual influence, which they expressed in practical ways. They succeeded through strength, not force. The only instrument of power at their disposal was cursing and expulsion from the community—the worst possible punishment for both an individual and for the whole tribe.

This sketch gives a rough outline of the role which the druids played between 700 and 300 BC. This was their heyday. At that time there was no hard and fast rule as to what was good and what was bad. The druids did not regard themselves as exalted mediators between the visible and the invisible world. Water, trees, wind, nature itself were there to do that job. Those were their church, and every Celt served them.

This all changed when the druids became fascinated by the temporally more precise prophecies from the East. Only a few druids in far-flung areas continued to proclaim the unity of life. The druid community survived above all in Ireland. But even there the druids of the old school retreated and allowed themselves to be outstripped by Saint Patrick. Ideologies come and go, but the druids' perception of the world goes on forever.

THE CELTIC TREE CALENDAR

Just as today there are many other calendars, quite apart from those of the Christian, Jewish, Muslim, Chinese and Indian cultures, so the different Celtic tribes also had divisions of time which initially were

regional variations regarding the classification of
each guardian tree. But common to all were connec-
tions with, first of all, the cycle of the moon and then
the course of the sun.

The moon calendar consists of a year made up
of 13 months of 28 days, that is 364 days. Each month
bears the name of a tree, which also stands for one of
the consonants of the Celtic 'tree alphabet':

1	Birch month	24.12–20.1	B-eth
2	Rowan month	21.1–17.2	L-uis
3	Weeping ash month	18.2–17.3	N-ion
4	Alder month	18.3–14.4	F-arn
5	Willow month	15.4–12.5	S-aille
6	Hawthorn month	13.5–9.6	H-uath
7	Oak month	10.6–7.7	D-uir
8	Holm oak month	8.7–4.8	T-inne
9	Hazel month	5.8–1.9	C-oll
10	Vine month	2.9–29.9	M-uin
11	Ivy month	30.9–27.10	G-ort
12	Blackthorn month	28.10–24.11	P-eith
13	Elder month	25.11–22.12	R-uis

The five vowels A, O, U, E and I gave the corresponding tree names to the nights of the solstices
and the equinoxes:

The night of the noble fir	21 December	A-ilm
The night of the gorse bush	21 March	O-nn
The night of the heather	21 June	U-ra
The night of the white poplar	23 September	E-adha
The 'secret' night of the yew		I-dho

Armed with this information we can easily imagine ourselves as a young Celt who wanted to know how his parents kept track of time. He would already have known these trees. With the help of their names he learned the Beth-Luis-Nion, the Celtic alphabet composed of 13 consonants and five vowels. And with the help of the consonants he counted the nights from the appearance of the thinnest crescent moon to the full moon, which reached its full size on the fourteenth night. One night, Ah! or Oh!, then a further 13 nights until the moon disappeared from the heavens for three nights, I, U and E—then the cycle began all over again.

The Celtic alphabet, or the Beth-Luis-Nion, can therefore serve as a list of numbers with which to count the duration of a phase of the moon. Twice the list of consonants plus four of the five vowels gives a round figure of 30 nights for one phase of the moon ($29\frac{1}{2}$ days). The vowel I is probably used for the night which is added to make it fit in better with

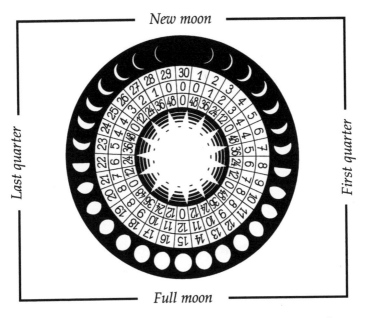

The moon inspired our ancestors, not to arithmetic, but to counting and recounting. So we know that it takes 29 to 30 days from full moon to full moon (29.53059 to be precise)!

the solar year. For a year has at least 365 days and not 13 times 28, which is 364.

In the construction of the Celtic tree circle we find 29 'Egyptian weeks' (the Egyptians originally divided the year into 36 large weeks of 10 days and one small week of five days) and the question is: where does the number 29 come from? The Celts certainly knew the solar month, the time span between two consecutive transits of the moon of the meridian of the vernal equinox. It lasts for just over 27 days. On the other hand, they were also certainly familiar with the synodic month, the time span between two similar phases of the moon. This lasts for about 29 days. We could be satisfied with that. But whilst we are wondering why the period of the walnut tree lasts for 19 days, the yew, which has been driven out, steps into the breach. The yew takes up nine days. Thus the walnut has only ten days left and instead of just 29, we now have 30 periods of ten days. This fits in well with the number three, the favourite number of the Celts. So we have 300 days accounted for. Then we have the time assigned to the poplar: a short week in February (five days), 14 days in May (a fortnight) and nine days in August; which together make 28 days. The elm has 13 days in January, which is the number of consonants in the Beth-Luis-Nion, and 11 in July. Now all we need are the nine 'secret' days of the yew and one day each for the oak, the birch, the olive and the beech, and we have all 365 days.

29 'Egyptian weeks' of 10 days each	= 290 days
3 'poplar periods' of 5 + 14 + 9 days	= 28 days
2 'elm periods' of 13 + 11 days	= 24 days

2 periods made up of the walnut's 10 days + the yew's 9 days	=	19 days
4 days for the oak, the birch, the olive and the beech	=	4 days
40 periods	total	365 days

The tree circle was much more than just a calendar for the Celts. It was a system of ordering so that knowledge of different kinds could be stored and recalled on several levels. Take, for example, the word for oak, *duir*. It was not just one well-defined concept, but opened up a larger sphere of meaning in which everything known in connection with the oak came to mind. It is a spontaneous natural force which renews itself perpetually, a symbol of wide distribution, supporting life, holding out a promise of happiness. In the Beth-Luis-Nion it gives its name to the month with the longest days. In the tree circle it marks the beginning of spring, the day when light and darkness are equal all over the world. Consequently it combines optimum tolerance and the greatest strength in the most beautiful balance.

The Celts liked to boast about their 'oak history'. Their longest bridge was called the 'oak bridge' not just because it was presumably built of oak, but also because it was the longest. If your herd of pigs produced the most piglets, then the oak was favourably disposed towards you. Knowledge of pig husbandry was learnt by heart under the 'chapter' of the oak. Anyone who knew it thoroughly was more successful and could exchange the surplus for gold. Consequently, knowledge of the extraction of gold and its processing was learnt in connection with the oak.

Ivy twines upwards on the oak, giving its name to the month between 30 September and 27 October, which sees store cupboards filled to overflowing. But the ivy also has a tendency to suppress the mistletoe which grows with it on the oak, just as affluence tends to suppress the good in men.

And so we come to the ethical level of the circle of associations of the oak. Strength, happiness and abundance should serve all. This is what the holy oak reminds us of, and the holy branch of the mistletoe which is cut by the white-robed druids with a golden knife at the festival of the oak.

The extent of knowledge revealed here by the example of the oak also holds good for each of the other trees in the tree circle. Understood in this way, it is a system of initiation which opens everybody's eyes to how everything in life is interwoven with everything else to form one complete whole.

THE TREES
OF
THE CELTIC CALENDAR

THE OAK
symbol of the life force

The oak (*Quercus*) is one of the wonders of nature. Its splendid appearance perfectly reflects the essence of this tree. With its strong, deep roots, short, thickset trunk, solid and elegantly swaying branches and broad, spreading crown, the oak withstands the centuries. All kinds of mosses live on it, clinging plants twine upwards around it. It bears this placidly and forms very hard wood throughout its life.

It grows best and reaches its fullest height in soil that is slightly damp and rich in humus, but it holds its own just as well in rocky ground. Its roots force their way inexorably through the cracks to find water. In some places it may only grow into a shrub, but that doesn't matter. The main thing is, it lives and produces leaves.

Old oak trees—they can be 500 years old, sometimes twice that—may be hollow or rotten inside, quite dead on one side and growing well on the other. If cockchafers or caterpillars eat away the leaves in spring, new bright green leaves grow again in June and July. Not even a felled oak tree will give up. Its wood survives for generations, living on

as wine or brandy barrels, as a table or a railway sleeper, the pier of a bridge or a ship afloat.

In the eighth century, when half of Europe was covered in oak groves, the apostle Boniface cut down a sacred oak in order to prove to the pagan Germans that their god was worthless since he couldn't even protect a tree. Then the oak became the tree of devils. Only the witches, who gathered there beneath it on Walpurgis Night before the first of May, remained faithful to it, protecting and worshipping it at the risk of their lives. They were burnt at the stake in fires of oak wood.

Wherever the oak grows there is always plenty of light for everything that grows around it and is sheltered by it. Perhaps oak trees remember their own youth, when they enjoyed and needed the protection and shade of other trees. They are often, for example, planted near lime trees until they are big enough. Then their 'foster mothers' are cut down. The oak does not forget that. It 'knows' that everything big and strong starts life as something small and weak. That is why it doesn't mutter when a gentle wind caresses its leaves. Nor does it howl when a storm tears at its branches. The oak always proclaims its wholehearted contentment with life. Who wouldn't want that as their native tree?

If you were born on 21 March you may, no you must, liken yourself to the oak. For you are endowed with the same indestructible vitality and strength of purpose. You like a fresh wind in every relationship and your vitality bursts into flames at any opposition. Your body may not live to be a thousand years old, but your soul lives on in your children and in your work. And if even the slightest drop of Celtic blood flows in your veins, then you will fear neither death nor devil. So what matters to you is not how long you live, but rather how intensively and meaningfully you fill your time.

The universe is God's plaything. You very happily agree to join the game. You put failures behind you and will seize the first favourable opportunity to prove yourself in new enterprises.

Of course, you can't help behaving like the farm lad who made a pact with the devil. 'You can have my soul when this oak no longer has any leaves,' he said. The devil agreed, but he waited in vain. For many oaks keep their old leaves over the winter, until the new buds burst into leaf in the spring. Don't you do the same thing? You prefer to cling to the old, well-tried methods until you have a clear understanding of the new, above all in 'winter' time. Or are you the sort of person who invests when the coffers are empty, and saves when they are over-flowing? Be careful, these are trick questions intended to provoke you. You like that, don't you?

You may be quite different from the sketch I have given here. Each human being is a unique individual. And not just people. Every oak tree is different, whether it is an English oak, a holm oak, a red oak or a swamp oak; each one seizes a unique opportunity to become what it is.

The Celts associated the strength to be oneself, which is latent in every person, with the oak. The truly strong man is he who has travelled a long way on the road to himself. Utterly dedicated, of his own free will he serves mankind, a cause, an art, responsible only to himself and full of the joy of living. He sees himself as the living instrument of God's power and does not lose himself in human reason, which thinks itself so dreadfully important.

Probably two to three thousand years ago there were relatively few people in whom the fire of the oak burned. But this is not the reason why the oak gives its name only to one day, like the beech, the olive tree and the birch. On the contrary, this limitation of time should make it stand out from the ranks of the other trees. It has been chosen to remind us, at the time of the vernal equinox on 21 March, that we should kindle a fire in ourselves that will allow us to find ourselves.

Native of the oak: Johann Sebastian Bach.
Gem stone: The ruby, which expresses a love of life.
Number: 3.
Medicinal use: A decoction of the bark helps cure acne.
Motto: Moderation in all things!

THE HAZEL
the tree that wants to be first

Hazels (*Corylus*) often grow in groups as bushes, but with plenty of sunshine and good, loamy soil a bush can occasionally grow into a tree with several trunks. For example, the Turkish hazel can have a trunk two metres (six feet) in circumference and up to 25 metres (80 feet) high.

This is the exception that proves the rule. In Central Europe the hazel is widespread as a bush and a favourite with young people, for it never carries its nuts too high. At the end of September or the beginning of October, depending on the amount of sun, the nuts begin to turn brown. They are edible as soon as they can be easily removed from their green covering, but a much more certain way of telling is when they are overrun by squirrels.

Scarcely has the hazel lost its nuts when it starts to form male catkins for the next year. They wait eagerly for the first warm days. Often they open as early as January and are frosted. Never mind—the main thing is that the hazel is the first to flower. These impatient male harbingers of spring are called 'lambs' tails', and the small, red, star-shaped, female flowers, which sit on the buds without stalks, are

called 'red styles'. The nuts develop from these. The hazel is clearly a self-fertile plant, since male and female organs can be found on the same bush, so the plant can fertilise and reproduce itself. This is one reason why it grows everywhere. It fights its way out from the densely populated heart of the wood to the edge, to the lighter places where it offers an endless bounty of nuts.

In the mountains it confines itself to the region of the oak (1,400–1,500 metres (4,600–5,000 feet) above sea level), not because of the height, but because it doesn't thrive as well in close company with beeches, firs and pines as it does in a mixed wood.

The hazel does not stand out either for its beauty or its size, and in the countryside it is as common as sparrows. But in folklore it has many roles to play. Things that have been lost can be found again, thanks to the fungi that grow on it. The mistletoe that grows on the hazel protects against bewitching. If you sleep under a hazel bush you will have vivid dreams. A hazel switch is no longer the teacher's staff of office, but divining rods are always cut from it. Anyone who wants to find water, precious metal or buried treasure needs a three-year-old forked twig from a hazel bush. It must not be cut with a knife, but with a flint.

The wonderful powers of the hazel should not be interpreted in a materialistic sense. Rather they have a spiritual relationship with the seasons, for the days of the hazel coincide with the ninth full moon after the summer and winter solstices. Those are the dates when sunlight conquers the darkness. Think of the midnight sun in the far north and the time at Christmas when the days start to get longer again.

If you were born during the days of the hazel (22–31 March and 24 September–3 October) then you were conceived nine months before, during the longest or shortest nights of the year.

Your tree of life, the hazel, is dedicated to the white goddess of sensuality and fertility. For just as a baby grows for nine months in its mother's womb, so a hazel grows for nine years in the womb of Mother Nature before it can produce nuts. So, if you tend to be impatient, put your trust in the number nine or in the rhythm of nine: nine hours, nine days, nine weeks, nine months or nine years—everything, big or small, needs time to renew itself. Don't be too hasty. Learn to value what is old. Those who despise what has already stood the test of time will miss something special. How quickly the stimulus of the new palls when we do not let it take root in us.

The hazel is a pioneering plant: it prepares the ground where nothing grows for the plants that will come after it. You too have the soul of a pioneer, but you waste too much energy on competitive thoughts and in fighting abuses instead of letting your own 'nuts' ripen. In reality, the man who is first is not the one who beats all the competition in the field, but the one who encourages and supports competition through his performance.

Natives of the hazel: Mahatma Gandhi, Brigitte Bardot.
Gem stone: Red spinel, which gives zest for life.
Number: 9.
Medicinal use: Tea made from the catkins promotes sweating and relieves congestion in the kidneys.
Motto: Love is the bud from which loyalty blossoms.

THE ROWAN
the favourite of the birds

The rowan belongs to the genus *Sorbus*, which includes about 80 different forms. The white-beam, the Hupeh rowan and the wild service tree, which was also called the 'griping service tree' because its berries could stop diarrhoea, also belong to this genus. The berries of the different types of rowan have many uses.

Apple or pear wine, when mixed with rowan berries, will be a little sharper but much stronger and have better keeping qualities. Rowanberry brandy cures stomach and intestinal chills or cramps. Those who have the time and patience can make a compote or jam to cure a hangover.

The rowan is also useful for its wood. It is hard and tough, and at the same time very pliable. It takes stains well and, highly polished, it shines strikingly beautifully. Difficult to split and not prone to fading, it was used by wood turners and wood carvers to make wooden screws, wheels and works of art. Not so long ago, shuttles in the weaving industry were made of rowan wood in preference to all others.

The rowan is just about the only deciduous

tree that grows up to the tree line, in company with the Norway spruce. In the mountains it is found as a many-stemmed bush in totally inaccessible places. Birds distribute its indigestible seeds over a wide area. In good chalky and clay soil and under the best conditions it grows to a height of 20 metres (66 feet), but it seems to care more about coping with life and being useful than about growing big and powerful. Trees five to ten metres (16 to 33 feet) high gracefully adorn the verges of our mountain roads. They tend to grow upwards rather than outwards. Long and lanky to begin with, they form domed crowns over the years. With their graceful foliage and shining red to orange berries they make good ornamental trees for parks and gardens. They do not take the light away from other trees.

In folklore the rowan is regarded as the god-mother of milch cows. When a calf is due to be named, the farmer goes to the wood before daybreak to cut a rowan branch with a piece of sheet copper just as the sun rises. He smacks the calf on the back with it and calls it by its name. After that he tethers it to the cowshed door, decorated with white ribbons and eggshells.

This tradition, which links the rowan's power to heal the stomach with the easy digestibility of milk, comes from the Celts who planted rowans at

that time of year when nature has not quite got rid of its 'eggshells'. Between 1 and 10 April nature is still in what is known as its 'babyhood' and needs looking after. In autumn (4–13 October), the rowan with its magnificent red and yellow leaves gives a vigilant early warning of approaching winter.

If you were born during the days of the rowan (1–10 April and 4–13 October) you will have a burning desire to brighten up the world and make it better. Relationships between people are what matter most to you, and the older you get the greater the contribution you will make in the service of your environment.

The way you manage to avoid becoming dependent on your fellow men is admirable. Instead of continually demanding recognition, as many others would do, you work consistently on 'brightening up' and bettering yourself. So you are seldom at a loss, even when you lack success and recognition. At the very least you have the pleasure of your own achievements. The motto 'Make yourself better, then you can make the world better' sums up your attitude to life.

Worthy though this is, it has its dangers. It may be that you are working so hard to perfect yourself that you will become isolated. Loneliness of any kind does not agree with you. It upsets you, it makes you sad, and often, standing out as you do from your surroundings, it can even make you unsure whether you are living in harmony with yourself. You are happier hiding your light under a bushel or taking responsibility for anything that goes wrong.

Sooner or later you will realise that worrying about the loss of others' love and sympathy is making you go too far. In certain circumstances this fear also stops you from fully finding yourself.

It would be a good idea for someone like you, who is so sensitive to harmony, to have daily discussions with their partner and the people close to them. Making concessions, which only involves one side, waters down life. Conflict seasons it.

It is up to you to make sure that those nearest to you are gradually made aware how unbearable they often are. Then they will value your love even more. Quietly attach conditions to the love and sympathy that you offer. The rowan, your tree of life, does not give away its fruit unquestioningly like a mother. It wants its hard, indigestible seeds to be scattered abroad!

Natives of the rowan: Le Corbusier, Eleanor Roosevelt.
Gem stone: Rhodochrosite, which unites people.
Number: 60.
Medicinal use: Tea made from the leaves helps diarrhoea.
Motto: Personal vanity is good if it motivates us to keep fit.

THE MAPLE
a quarrelsome angel?

The maple (*Acer*) is often called the 'angel's head tree' because its winged seeds fly down from the top of its crown like angels, fluttering round and round. This name is quite unworthy of this imposing tree which grows to a height of up to 30 metres (100 feet) in 60 to 80 years. But the contradiction between this name and its appearance is really quite apt. For while the maple loves the mountains, it is not really suited to the hard struggle for life in that rugged climate. In higher areas it suffers much more from the wind and snow and brittleness in its frozen branches than do conifers, beeches or oaks. And yet it still tries to imitate those trees. In mixed timber woods it copies the pines and grows tall and straight, like they do, with a small crown.

Growing in isolation it sends down a root system as strong and well-developed as the oak. But its crown, with its thick foliage, tries to withstand much more punishment from the wind than its trunk can take. As low as ground level or just above it, the trunk frequently splits in two and thus weakens its weight-bearing capacity. Nevertheless the powerful branches sweep out in elegant curves, soaring upwards. It simply refuses to grow straight. It stubbornly twists, turns and crosses over itself on its way upwards. There is hardly a straight branch or twig to be found on a maple.

Nobody knows how long a maple can live. It is estimated at 150–200 years. But a mighty maple, under which the local authorities who founded the Grey League met in 1424, stood in the town of Truns in Bündner until 117 years ago. So the maple must live to be as old as the oak. Only in those instances where people associate their history with a tree does sentiment triumph over considerations of usefulness and profit.

The wood of the maple shines white like an angel. But it only stays white if it is cut down in winter and immediately split and the planks placed upside down. What was at the top of the tree must be at the bottom of the planks. 'The wood of the maple is as white as snow, but as transitory as the snow that falls in April,' said the druids. They also noticed how frequently it grew with two trunks and so they let twice ten days pass between the days of the oak and the beginning of the maple's days. These last from 11 to 20 April. In autumn they liked to draw some of the sap from the maple. It tastes slightly sweet and cools fiery temperaments. Tea made from maple leaves also has a calming effect.

In general the 'five-fingered leaves' express the relationship between people and the tree. Five trees follow the maple in autumn (14–23 October), then comes the day of the beech, the tree of necessity, one of the four anchors of the tree circle. The natural

phenomena of the tree world are closely linked with
the 'nature' of natural numbers. They weren't there
just as numbers but were worshipped as messengers
of the divine order.

If you were born during the days of the maple
you will not be completely satisfied with obvious
answers. That is why the struggle for identity is so
important to you. You can do without certainty,
comfort and many other things, but you cannot do
without the recognition or prestige in the community which you feel is your due.

Whatever you do, say or think is the expression of your own will. And this desire for independence frequently gets in the way of your need for
give-and-take. You are the one who suffers most
from that, not those around you. You admire people
who assert themselves clearly and consistently. You
overlook their harshness and thoughtlessness, either

because you often demand very high standards of yourself or because you love a challenge. This is why you welcome with open arms anything you don't know, the strange, even the hostile. You need that for your personal development. But, unlike you, those around you don't want to deal openly and honestly with conflict and grow from this experience, and you don't want to go ahead without their approval. As an impatient, dynamic person, you can be amazingly patient while trying to convince those around you of what has long been clear to you, since you fearlessly face up to anything new. If you lived alone you would have attained paradise a long time ago.

People who were born during the days of the maple stand out because of their strong determination, their sense of community and their untiring and committed activity.

Natives of the maple: Alfred Nobel, Peter Ustinov, Charlie Chaplin, Oscar Wilde, Anatole France, Nikita Khrushchev.
Gem stone: The red carnelian, which calms anger.
Number: 7.
Medicinal use: The bruised leaves soothe the inflammation of insect bites.
Motto: He who is strong looks after the weak.

THE WALNUT
searching for its homeland

The original home of the walnut (*Juglans*) that grows in Europe probably lies somewhere in the region from between the Black Sea and the Caspian Sea as far as the Persian Gulf. On the sunny slopes of the foothills of the Caucasus they grow in such numbers that they even form woods. But as early as the time of the great migration of peoples the walnut had spread from there across Greece and Italy to France and beyond into our latitude. The Celts also brought it to Britain and Ireland. Today we see these beautiful broad-crowned trees growing out in the open countryside, in gardens, even on sheltered hills on the North European coast, but never where the soil is sandy.

Without its leaves the crown appears sparse. With its leaves it is a well-developed shade tree which allows nothing to grow beneath it. Its foliage is thick because heavily-leaved twigs sprout all along the branches, even within the crown.

The trunk of the walnut tree is relatively short. Two or three metres (six or ten feet) from the ground it usually divides into several massive branches. It is grained and gnarled as well, and in

old age almost always hollow. In 60 years the tree grows to about 20 metres (65 feet), and about 30 metres (98 feet) after 100 years. Its wood is tough and flexible, with lighter and darker shades running through it. Curiously enough, diseased wood with knobbled veins running through is very highly prized in the furniture industry. These nodules are swellings of the trunk caused by fungi, bacteria and other diseases. On the other hand, insects neither harm this tree, nor are they of use to it. The plant is self-fertile, though it also lets the wind pollinate it. Climate is its only potential danger. It needs a lot of sunshine and is sensitive to the cold. If the frosts at the end of April catch the flowers there will be no nuts to harvest. St Mark's Day, 25 April, was therefore feared by walnut tree growers even more than a cold spell in the middle of May. It was certainly not accidental that the Celts paid particular attention to walnut trees on the days between 21 and 30 April. And dedicating 19 whole days to this tree in autumn, from 24 October to 11 November, shows how much they valued walnuts. With their high fat and protein content they supplied the ideal food for the onset of the winter cold.

But this unusually long period of time also highlighted their deepest concerns. For the Celts gloried in the magnificent colours of the trees and woods in autumn, whose splendour was cut short by the first November storms. The walnut tree briefly stood there in all its glory, in full leaf, covered in nuts, yet in one night all that richness, all that power was blown away. Where the proud crown had been, there was now just a thin skeleton of branches and twigs. This annual death of nature made them aware of the transience of all things, and so 1 November was the most important of their four festivals of the year. On that day they drank beer and ate roast goose stuffed with walnuts. For us this became All Souls Day.

Pleasure or pain, profit or loss? Clearly these questions shuffle the cards of your life, openly or otherwise, if you were born during the days of the walnut tree. We could say that of everybody. But only 'walnut people' are capable of so much passion in safeguarding or defending their zest for life. No sacrifice is too great in your struggle to retain what you hold dear. It sounds so paradoxical: you are ready to suffer all that pain for the sake of pleasure. Yet you hardly ever manage to succeed in that. Nevertheless you are envied by the majority who avoid questioning themselves too seriously, because your life has depth and piquancy and frequently bears an abundance of fruit. If you do something, you do it wholeheartedly. If you want something, your persistence knows no bounds. If you love something, then this love lasts until death. This unequivocal attitude is linked to the power of your unconscious. You know instinctively what Martin Luther meant when he said, 'Here I stand. I can do no other. God help me!'

Keep your eye on the yew as well, if you were born between 3 and 11 November. It stands in the mysterious shadows behind the passion of the walnut tree.

Natives of the walnut: William Shakespeare, Dylan Thomas, Pablo Picasso, Vladimir Nabokov, Queen Elizabeth II.
Gem stone: Serpentine, which banishes homesickness.
Number: 16.
Medicinal use: Crushed walnut leaves are an effective insect repellent.
Motto: So you're living in a rut. Why worry about it?

THE POPLAR
the tree that overcomes uncertainty

The genus *Populus* includes more than 30 species, divided into three or four groups. But the different kinds cross-pollinate so easily that it is very difficult to tell which one is which.

The one most widely known is the Lombardy poplar. It hugs all its branches to itself and looks like an elongated forefinger pointing high into the sky. It did not grow like this in the time of the Celts. This mutation only came into being in the middle of the eighteenth century in northern Italy. It cannot be propagated from seed, like the white poplar or the other varieties, only from cuttings.

If you take a twig and push it into the ground a new tree will grow from it. You won't have to wait long because poplars are our fastest-growing source of timber. Napoleon used them, planting them all along his military roads. They are so widespread in Europe today that we tend to forget the black and white poplars, and even the strongly scented balsam poplars. But we cannot ignore the sound of the poplars. The slightest breeze sets the long-stemmed leaves rustling, especially those of the aspen, and in a wind they sound like a rushing waterfall.

The wood of the poplar is very light, soft and pale, easy to carve and hollow out. Even in Celtic times it was used to make clogs, but its chief importance was as wood for the shields with which the Celts protected themselves in battle. Leather was stretched over them, hardened and made durable by tanning with poplar bark. Today poplar wood is used in the manufacture of cellulose and for making plywood and matches.

Because of the changes in the poplar over the years, its natural characteristics and its many uses, it gave its name not just to two, but to three periods in the Celtic calendar—4–8 February, 1–14 May and 5–13 August. In February its dark brown buds swell so vigorously that the entire tree appears full of them. In May its leaves are reddish brown, contrasting beautifully with the May green of other trees. In summer they appear either white, black or strikingly light green, depending on the species—but as we have said, it is difficult to distinguish clearly between the different kinds of poplar.

The Celts were as unsure as we are, and the days of the poplar are an uncertain time for the majority of plants that we need in our lives. The increase in light in February, mirrored by the rapid growth of the poplar, often stimulates impatience in us. Can we then blame the plants for

thinking that maybe spring is here? In any case, uncertainty dominates this time of year. No one can be sure that winter will not return again in full force.

Uncertainty also rules in May. The late frosts are not yet over. And in August thunderstorms, lightning and hail can destroy the harvest. How, then, can we conquer our own doubts?

This question is important to all those born during the days of the poplar, and the tree itself may provide part of the answer: it grows quickly. Poplar people learn quickly, thanks to their quick intelligence. Their spirit is as agile as the wood of the tree is malleable. But they are not happy-go-lucky. On the contrary, like the poplar they spread their roots wide and deep in the soil that nourishes them. Those in charge of public parks avoid planting poplars because their roots quickly reach out and grow round water mains and pipes sunk deep in the ground.

Poplar people quietly ensure that they are firmly in the saddle. They lavish care and attention on their relationships, and those they trust can depend on them. They are generous when approached. They don't exploit anybody nor do they let anyone exploit them. Clever like the poplar, they survive by seeking and using every possible opportunity.

Did you know that your tree of life, the poplar, 'sweats out', so to speak, one hundred per cent of all the water that it absorbs? Have you too conquered your uncertainty to such an extent that you do not feel the need to build up large reserves?

If those around you are unsympathetic and lacking in affection, you hold back, but in a warm, friendly atmosphere you are outgoing and very receptive to new things and new people. Your sense of moderation, a characteristic you share with the poplar, is one of the weapons you use to overcome the uncertainty of life—not to mention your varied interests and your corresponding willingness to make contacts and communicate. People can talk to you about anything and discuss anything, so long as they don't go too far. You are only hostile to closed minds, extremists or those who think they have found the philosopher's stone.

You should also take note of the description of the yew (*Taxus*).

Natives of the poplar: Florence Nightingale, Henri Dunant, Mata Hari.
Gem stone: Coral, which creates good relationships.
Number: 5.
Medicinal use: Tea made from the buds helps bladder complaints and prostate problems.
Motto: Those who promise too much can deliver very little.

THE CHESTNUT
in quest of its truth

A s a distant relation of the oak, the chestnut (*Castanea*) combines the lightness of the beech with the beauty of the walnut tree.

To start with, we have to ask whether we are dealing with the sweet chestnut or the horse chestnut. The answer, according to the Celts, is the sweet chestnut, since this is the one that blooms at the end of May, around the period assigned to it in the calendar: 15–24 May.

The horse chestnut produces its magnificent flowers more than a month earlier. Its name in the old Indo-European language means 'false', 'artificial', so perhaps the 'false' chestnut made the Celts see the 'real' chestnut as a tree of honesty or even of truth. The two species can easily be distinguished by the difference in their leaves, flowers and fruits: the sweet chestnut has serrated, lance-shaped leaves of average size, whilst those of the horse chestnut are enormous finger-shaped plumes.

In spring the horse chestnut does not hang back like the other trees. It is soon resplendent in its magnificent leaves and flowers, with the colourful

flower candles giving it the appearance of a flam-
boyant chandelier.

The sweet chestnut, on the other hand, takes
its time and contents itself with long, loose, yellowy-
green catkins which hang like threads and among
which the female flowers are barely visible.

It's a known fact that the fruit of the horse
chestnut is palatable only to animals, because it contains large quantities of tannic acid and bitter sub-
stances. On the other hand, everyone loves roasting
sweet chestnuts in the fire when winter comes.

To be fair, it must be said that horse chestnuts
fresh out of their prickly shells are more beautiful
than sweet chestnuts. Like acorns, they were once
used as a coffee substitute and—instead of hops—to
brew beer. During fermentation a spirit is produced
which can cure a cough. Bookbinders and paper
hangers, too, use a paste made from horse chestnuts.

Perhaps it is the quality of wood which makes
it more likely that the Celts were thinking of the
sweet chestnut. In Mediterranean countries furniture made from its wood is highly prized. Often it is
difficult to tell it from oak, but it grows faster and
more strongly, is tougher, even easier to use and has
greater weight-bearing capacity. The wood of the
horse chestnut is used for carving. It takes colour
well and can be beautifully polished. What's more, it

doesn't appeal to worms. In the north coopers make staves from the wood of the horse chestnut, and in southern Europe they use sweet chestnut wood. The sweet chestnut will not grow in a harsh climate and needs good, deep soil which is not too damp and not too dry. Then it forms groves through which the light shines easily. In contrast to this the horse chestnut is well known as a shade tree, under which it remains cool and dark. Are you a sweet chestnut or a horse chestnut?

People born during the days of the chestnut (15–24 May and 12–21 November) are too self-critical to count themselves amongst the noble, useful or good. But falsehood is so foreign to your way of thinking that you prefer to stick with a mistake until you are absolutely sure it is a mistake. Sometimes, in consequence, you are accused of being stubborn. But this is to forget just how close truth and lies are to each other and how difficult it can be to separate the wheat from the chaff.

Those who believe in honesty must match words with deeds and keep going long enough in the direction they have chosen. Anyone who wavers will find only half the truth. But the success of your endeavours depends on serving not just honesty, but also good sense and, even better, humour. You could say that the truthful serious person has at his disposal an endless supply of humour which is never hurtful.

Chestnuts in particular are often cut back, and although they grow back again strongly, their natural shape is lost. That can also happen to you. So look for a chestnut tree that has grown naturally, away from a wood. It doesn't even have to be the 'noble' sweet chestnut. It is your tree of life. Under it you will find your truth.

Natives of the chestnut: Robert Louis Stevenson, Indira Gandhi, Auguste Rodin, Voltaire.
Gem stone: Jade, which keeps everything in a state of flux.
Number: 19.
Medicinal use: The bark of the shoots, mixed with water, protects against sunburn.
Motto: Everything we think we know is just supposition.

THE ASH
aspiring to the heights

O f the 60 or so types of ash, the one we know best is *Fraxinus excelsior*. Although it is called the 'common ash' this name does not suit it, for at 35 to 45 metres (115–150 feet) it is one of the tallest-growing deciduous trees. Yet it doesn't like growing in woodland situations, it is much happier at the edge of a beech wood and does best of all on a river bank as a loyal, friendly companion of sombre alders and English oaks, or just by itself.

Like the willows and poplars, the ash tolerates a great deal of mishandling, and can also be trained into any other shape to become, for example, a hanging or a weeping ash. The manna ash, a smaller tree with a more rounded crown which is particularly pretty in bloom, can be cut open and produces a substance which contains sugar and is known as 'manna'.

In days gone by ash trees were freely plundered by farmers. Not only twigs but entire branches were cut off so that the leaves could be used as animal fodder. It was said that goats that ate ash leaves never became ill. In natural healing, the leaves and

seeds were used to cure rheumatism and gout. A preparation was made from the bark for use against fever or to heal wounds.

The light brown wood of the ash is hard, tough, and above all durable and flexible. The Celts used it to make spears, lances, bows and arrows. Today, castles often stand where the Celts had their fortresses. Traditionally, ash trees were planted in the surrounding area. Now we no longer use them for weapons, but for gymnastic equipment of all kinds, and for skis and walking sticks.

The druids attributed special powers over water to the ash tree. They used its wood to make it rain or to ward off water's destructive power. In fact, the incredibly long roots of the ash can strengthen embankments, an inestimable help in June when rivers are swollen by melting snow from the mountains. But it wasn't just this natural phenomenon that led the druids to consecrate the days from 25 May to 3 June and 22 November to 1 December to the ash. The ash itself was the decisive factor because it marks the transition from the merry month of May to June. Frost-sensitive as it is, it waits until no more frost is expected.

Not until after the middle of May, which can be particularly cold, and towards the end of May and the beginning of June, when most trees are already turning a darker green, does the ash completely unfurl its charming feathery leaves and gleam light green until the autumn, when the first frost makes the leaves fall. At the end of November, when many trees still have a few colourful leaves, the ash is already completely leafless, showing branches and twigs all straining upwards.

People born in the days of the ash seek their fortune in the upper echelons of society. Many of them have been 'condemned' for being ambitious and stubborn or calculating. But they are simply trying to improve their situation in life. Perhaps it was the ash's tendency to search out and exhaust the friable, cultivated earth with its roots which prompted this scathing judgement.

More than anyone else, ash people take care of the morrow and will sacrifice many cherished desires if their goal demands it. Their main objective is identity, freedom and independence, and to achieve this end they are ready to risk everything. For this they are capable of sacrificing themselves completely. It is this willingness, not luck, that enables them to reach their goal.

People who have the ash as their tree of life appear to know instinctively that they must first go through a hell of imprisonment in order to reach their heaven. In spite of grumbles and complaints they are capable of serving a cause or a person loyally for many years. Very few other people can put up with being kept down for so long in order to reach the heights. True greatness may appear when 'ashes' reach their peak and they stay 'on top' for as long as they were kept down. But now this is no longer just for them and those close to them. The farther they have got, the harder they struggle to help as many of their fellow men as possible to freedom and independence.

Living with people of this type is certainly no simple matter, unless one works as hard as they do to develop one's own individuality. They can teach us how to develop our own powers of judgement which might then be accepted as general guidelines. Those born during the days of the ash have little faith in authority, so they are only called upon as a last resort, when established opinions have failed.

When things are really in a mess 'ash trees' put them back onto a safe, well thought-out track.

Natives of the ash: Charles de Gaulle, Winston Churchill, John F. Kennedy, Henry Kissinger.
Gem stone: The fire opal, which reminds everyone of vulnerability.
Number: 22.
Medicinal use: Tea made from ash leaves relieves rheumatism and gout.
Motto: Power is linked with mistrust, strength with trust.

THE HORNBEAM
a monument to loyalty

T he wood of the hornbeam (*Carpinus*) used to be called 'iron wood'. It is the hardest European tree used for timber and grows in any soil.

The hornbeam is close to the heart of those who still know what it means to be loyal to their fellow men and to nature. It is an inconspicuous tree, which makes no great demands and gives its services everywhere. In coppices it can be cut down every 15 to 30 years and springs up again as strongly as ever from stumps a hundred years old.

As early as Celtic times the hornbeam was protecting farmsteads by forming impenetrable hedgerows round them, and enclosures into which cattle were driven. Planted close together, they took the place of ramparts. Its wood is as hard and as tough as that. Not long ago it was used for coach-building, for cider presses, gun carriages—in short, for everything that had to be reliably hard and long-lasting, like the 'morning stars', the flails used by the early Swiss people.

The hornbeam has not survived to the present day just because it forms thickset hedges which give

protection against prying eyes even in winter—the leaves generally stay on the tree until early in the year; on the contrary, without us it would undoubtedly have spread even further. For it sneaks in unobtrusively all over the place and establishes itself in even the most inhospitable places with amazing tenacity. Even in dark coniferous forests it outlasts generations of conifers, misshapen it is true, but always ready to fill any gaps. You wouldn't think that a tree that needed light would be able to do this. It also survives in impoverished, dry soil as a bush and in locations which are particularly exposed to late frosts. It is so independent of nature and so faithful in its service to mankind! That is why the Celts spoke highly of the loyal hornbeam, which served them faithfully even when it received nothing but disadvantages in return.

The hornbeam takes its place in the tree circle from 4 to 13 June and from 2 to 11 December. In June it is particularly distinctive thanks to its grape-shaped bunches of seeds, which are so big and so numerous that they quickly hide the leaves and decorate the tree with a vivid light green colour well into October or even November. In December the leaves are still on the hornbeam, which is among the few trees that can successfully defy the November storms.

If these trees do fail to keep their leaves we can marvel at their interesting shapes from the roots to the crown: under the ground, numerous roots spread out from the trunk. The bark remains youthfully smooth right into old age. It is very flexible and withstands the great swelling of the trunk. The shape of the branches in old trees is extraordinarily twisted, turning to and fro in sharp angles, almost like the oak. In young trees the branches grow densely upwards in sharp angles. Soon it is no longer round like a cylinder, but full of rounded corners, with bumps, bulges and knots to delight the curious.

People who were born during the days of the hornbeam will declare unhesitatingly that for them loyalty is a very important consideration. But hand on heart! Would you really put up with the disadvantages of remaining loyal to a disloyal partner or employer? Just to be able to remain true to yourself?

Whether or not you believe that, many 'hornbeams' instinctively assume responsibility for mistakes which should be blamed on their partner or their employer. What is attractive about this is that tolerance and the settling of disputes matter more to 'hornbeams' than rigid laws that demand scapegoats.

As a native of the hornbeam you have a very

good sense of what is fair. Justice, not equality, is your model. You do not expect everyone to be as clever, as strong or as sensitive as everyone else. But they should all have the same chances to find out what their potential is. A lot of feeling, a strong, clear will and a readiness to yield in order to preserve a proper moderation—those are the prerequisites for all fair behaviour and judgement.

If the hornbeam is your tree of life, then at least you are blessed with a talent for bringing rather more justice into our lives. This is why you scorn sweeping judgements or dismiss fanaticism as laughable and avoid squabbles over who is right. If this doesn't work, you just accept that people are being unfair to you. When others make a scene you forgive them generously. You prefer to suffer injustice yourself than to be unfair to others; your sense of honour won't let you.

If you think that I have drawn a picture that is

far too idealistic, you are quite right. You feel your-self obliged to accept this ideal, especially when you see that you are not able to comply with it. You are able, through 'failure', to go through with it. That means, you let hard wood grow.

A striking feature of the life of many promi-nent 'hornbeams' is this tension they had to endure between the ideal and hard reality.

Natives of the hornbeam: Mary, Queen of Scots, Alexander Solzhenitsyn, Rainer Maria Rilke, Thomas Mann, Maria Callas.
Gem stone: Yellow diamonds, which encourage relia-bility.
Number: 17.
Medicinal use: Dry leaves crumbled in the hand strengthen your courage to face life.
Motto: Revenge is one way of restoring the balance.

THE FIG
a very accommodating tree

Anyone who claims that the fig tree (*Ficus carica*) does not belong in the tree calendar underestimates the cosmopolitan nature of the Celts. They were curious, eager for travel and adventure, and not content just to eat one of the most appetising fruits of the Mediterranean in Turkey, Italy, Portugal or Greece. They took its seeds with them to Central Europe and Britain and tried to establish it there.

In warmer regions north of the Alps this plant just manages to survive the winter. But it grows there more as a bush than a tree, and very rarely sets edible fruit. No one can blame it for its sensitivity to early frosts and winter cold. On the contrary, it deserves the highest praise. It has achieved the impossible. Of about 700 types of fig that flourish in the tropics and sub-tropics, this is the only one that has developed the hardiness to cope with winter in our part of the world. We are also familiar with the *Ficus elastica*, the rubber plant, but that overwinters as a pot plant in heated rooms. It has earned it. Before synthetic rubber was discovered, it was one of the best known rubber trees.

All representatives of the genus *Ficus* exude a milky sap (latex) when their bark is cut. In some places this is still used in the manufacture of chewing gum. But now fig trees are grown just for their delicious or at least nutritious fruit, and therefore just as female specimens. Figs take many months to ripen. Most grow in the leaf axils, behind the leaves. So they sit directly on the branches or the trunk, or even form underground, like potatoes.

Several types of fig are called 'strangling figs'. They start life growing on other trees, sending countless air roots down to the earth. As a result the host tree soon dies. The 'strangler', for example the *Ficus bengalis*, then lives on, thanks to its own well-anchored roots. It develops large supporting roots like a forest of trunks. In India and throughout Indonesia grows a fig known as the *Ficus religiosa* which has great religious significance for Hindus and Buddhists. This one does not strangle anything!

The tree itself doesn't grow very tall. I have never seen any over five metres (16 feet). From just above ground level its branches grow in all directions, at first horizontally and then gently upwards. If the fruit has not been knocked down already, children can collect the figs by climbing up the trunk as though it were a spiral staircase. What other tree is so accommodating?

If your birthday falls between 14 and 23 June or 12 and 21 December, then the fig is your tree of life and your nature is related to that of the fig. Doesn't your sensitivity often make life seem harsh to you? You can't have one without the other. Anyone who has to put up with harshness really knows how to enjoy sweetness. Those who look only for sweetness find harshness intolerable.

Don't you often feel that the diversity of life is too much of you? People like you who let everything impress them should withdraw more often into the stillness in order to absorb everything that affects their senses. However, there are some people born during the days of the fig tree who can accept their sensitiveness and do not allow themselves to be continually at the mercy of each new impression.

The typical essential qualities of 'fig trees' can be found at every level of society. Lowly or great, they all have to decide whether to opt for sensitivity or lack of emotion. They have to decide whether to live purely creatively or as a parasite, sacrificing truth in favour of trickery.

This is easier said than done. But the strength needed to preserve human sensitivity in insensitive and unsettled times flows continuously from your roots. When somebody hurts you, you become aware of the vulnerability of others. When someone brings you something that makes an impression on you, then you learn that frequently silence is golden, even in a society founded on information.

Since you were born on one of the longest or shortest days, or one of the longest or shortest nights of the year, it is obviously more difficult for you than for others to find the right balance between feeling and reason, quietness and hectic rushing about, sweetness and harshness. Wavering first one way and then the other is a part of your life, as is occasional exaggeration. Only chronic imbalance or chronic exaggeration are dangerous to you.

Natives of the fig: Joseph Stalin, Jean-Paul Sartre, Françoise Sagan, Anne Frank, Willy Brandt.
Gem stone: The noble opal, which helps to overcome sensitivity.
Number: 20.
Medicinal use: Fingernails dipped in the juice of fig leaves become harder.
Motto: Every desire dies with its fulfilment, wanting spurs us on.

THE BIRCH
the tree of initiation

No deciduous tree is as winter-hardy as the birch (*Betula*).

Men have always been impressed by extremes in nature. Thousands travel every year to the far north in order to see with their own eyes that there is a place where the sun never sets. These are comfortable journeys. Nevertheless, nobody forgets the sight of the midnight sun.

The experience of the far north had a much deeper effect on the Celts. It meant long, arduous journeys on foot, beset by fear of the unknown. Then the promised wonder: the darkness of night failed to materialise. It is easy to see how Europe north of the Arctic circle became the land of divinities of light, the home of the white goddess and her birch groves. When they discovered that the birch tree survives for six months in summer without night and the same length of time in winter without day in the freezing cold, it earned their unquestioning admiration.

They made the birch the tree of light. Its holy day is celebrated on 24 June, three days after the summer solstice, just as we Christians celebrate the holy day three days after the winter solstice as Christmas.

Even those who usually stifle their feelings of love so that they can continue undisturbed with their scientific observations, have acknowledged the unusual abilities of this plant: its bark is full of air and guaranteed waterproof. It is incredibly robust. Pieces of birch bark hundreds of years old have been excavated intact from peat bogs.

The Indians of North America used it instead of leather to cover their canoes. Laplanders use it to make cloaks and leggings. The Norwegians cover their roofs with birch bark and a layer of earth. When everything else in the wood is wet you can still make a fire with a piece of birch bark. Waterproof leather, known as Russia leather, is tanned using its sap, which contains a great deal of sugar, oil and vitamin C.

The wood of the birch is very hard, strong and easy to work. Swiss alpenhorn players know this. In the furniture industry grained birch is particularly valued. But all types find a use as boxes, baskets, notepaper, plywood and veneers. It is popular as firewood because it burns with very bright flames and gives a lot of light.

In natural healing the sap of the birch is used

to regulate the water balance of the body. It stimulates the kidneys, removes acid and fat from the blood of those suffering from gout and rheumatism and cleans the skin. The Celts drank the sap as a beauty potion. Birch water still has this reputation in the cosmetics industry.

Usually a tree is even more impressive when it is old. This is not true of the birch. It is an enchanting tree in its youth, with an impressive grace and beauty which it retains for a long time. To the Celts the birch was the tree of the centre, just as the hazel was the tree of the beginning, and the alder was the tree of the approaching end.

In spring and summer it symbolises youth in full bloom. In autumn it edges this golden mean with its yellow-gold foliage; in winter it is the tree of the loving embrace of heaven and earth.

If you were born on 24 June you are always ready to help, even when it involves realising someone else's dream. Very often you are better at that than at fulfilling your own wishes.

You do a great deal for others and hope that others will also do something for you. With your highly developed community spirit, you will inevitably be disappointed sometimes. But you will remain as loyal to an idea as you will to an unfulfilled wish. You know how to wait, even though it

can be painful. Aware that wishes die as soon as they are fulfilled, you are careful to cultivate one of the most valuable feelings that exists: gratitude.

Those born on the day of the birch usually enjoy good health and remain cheerful, alert and appreciative all their lives. Even though they often rise to high positions, they remain modest. Only rarely do they fall victim to ambition or vanity. Either their intelligence or their intuition warns them against exaggeration of any kind.

Excess, tyranny or egotism only have a chance of coming to the fore if your rightful claims to dignity and respect were disregarded in childhood. Those who were born on the day of the birch and enjoyed the loving support of their parents and teachers are happy, as adults, to give back to the world three times as much encouragement as they received.

Let us not forget that the birch is a tree which

needs a great deal of light, which lets through a great deal of light and which only uses its fine side roots to exhaust all the nutrients around it when the soil is poor.

Natives of the birch: Othmar Kohler, the 'Doctor of Stalingrad', Manuel Fangio.
Gem stone: The emerald, which fortifies us in the sorrows of life.
Number: 2.
Medicinal use: Tea made from birch buds purifies the blood.
Motto: Beware of self-interest!

THE BEECH
the one who waits

The truly regal beech (*Fagus*) seems to have reached the end of its evolutionary journey, for the creative power, so evident in the other deciduous trees, in this one appears to be exhausted. Its close relative, the oak, numbers about 300 species, the beech just ten which, apart from the leaf form, are virtually indistinguishable.

Perhaps this restriction to what is necessary, this concentration on essentials, explains this tree's victory in the fight for supremacy in our woods. Unlike the oak, it does not cover its trunk and branches in a thick, corky layer. It makes do with a thin, silvery-grey bark which remains smooth and is sensitive to scorching by the sun. On the other hand, this forces it to form a canopy of leaves which completely blocks out the sunshine. Hardly any other deciduous tree produces such a perfect leaf cover.

A solitary beech will cover its trunk in branches and twigs from quite low down, but in the wild it forms a tall beech wood which sends back a mighty echo when you shout into it. It is like being in a cathedral in which you dare only whisper. Like vast pillars, the colossal trunks stand in close, regimented ranks, soaring to a dizzy height. There are no branches low down, just a crown forming a dark green 'dome' that hides the sky and permits nothing to grow under it. Tiny beech saplings doze there for decades until an old mother tree, rotten through and through, finally leaves a space free and a gap opens to let in some light. Beech trees have an implacable sense of what is necessary, even where their successors are concerned. All members of the species will assert themselves over others with ruthless persistence.

But the beech has worked hard to achieve its status as queen of the forest. It can thrive in poor, chalky soil where other trees find it heavy going. It is as thorough in its use of sunlight as it is in its penetration of damp ground with its surface roots. And it helps to keep itself moist with a dense covering of leaves which it produces every year. It doesn't just tolerate cool summers with very little sun, it actually likes cool, rainy conditions.

Nothing has a greater calorific value than hard beech wood. Experiments have shown that 14 cubic metres (494 cubic feet) of beech wood produce as much heat as 16 cubic metres (565 cubic feet) of oak. This alone explains why the beech has always been exploited by mankind. It wasn't just grown by charcoal burners, who used it to make charcoal. As the number of glassworks and iron foundries

increased, not only copper beeches 'paid with their lives'. Whole beech woods were cut down. Amid the euphoria of glass and steel during the last century, the fact that their nuts, the beechmast, are 40 per cent fat, and that half a litre (nearly a pint) of good salad oil can be extracted from a kilo (two pounds) of them, was overlooked.

The Celts were well aware that the beech was destined to assert itself in the long term. Along with the oak, the birch and the olive, it occupies one of the four 'milestones' of the solar year. Perhaps they simply compared the people who were born on this day, 22 December, with their tree of life, for are they not, like the beech, kings and queens in their own spheres? If they aren't, they can still become so. As we have seen, beech trees must spend long years in the shade before there is finally a place free for them to prove their worth. Far below, in the shadows of their elders, they are preparing for the future when they will fulfil their role. Patiently they wait until the time comes for them to take up the torch which their predecessors can no longer carry.

Are you as strict towards your own heirs as your tree of life is? Probably, for those who are too focused on the future are more easily seduced by the past than those who live completely in the present. This is particularly true of stern realists, among

whose ranks 'beeches' like to number themselves.

Think about all the conventions, rules, laws and criteria which in general we accept blindly. They all come from the past. We are very grateful for what our forefathers have handed down to us. But this won't stop those born on the day of the beech from questioning everything. As Goethe put it, we are 'an outstanding form, which develops by living'.

The following can be used as a test question to decide whether someone born on the day of the beech is ready to search for the right balance himself: "What isn't learnt as a child, will never be learnt as an adult.' Does that saying make sense to you?

Natives of the beech: Giacomo Puccini, Jean Racine.
Gem stone: The sapphire, which opens the way to wisdom.
Number: 4.
Medicinal use: The beech has never played much of a role in healing.
Motto: Beware of being useful to others!

THE APPLE
fulfilment in love

We could argue about whether Eve offered Adam a forbidden apple or a fig or even an orange. In any event the fruit didn't do him much good. And where did they find the fig leaves to cover that little difference which they were suddenly so ashamed of? Nobody knows.

To the Celts, who didn't know the Old Testament, the fig tree was the Tree of Knowledge of Good and Evil, not of Knowledge of the Differences between the Sexes to which we all owe our lives. The apple tree (*Malus*) was the symbol of perfection, the expression of the love that links nature and man, life and death, this world and the Other World.

No one dared touch the seven holy trees—the birch, the alder, the willow, the oak, the holm oak, the hazel and the apple—and to the fanatical missionaries that was a thorn in the flesh. The apple tree, called *Quert* in Celtic, was known as *Malus sylvestris* in Latin. In order to replace what they saw as a heathen cult with their own beliefs, these missionaries made the tree of love and immortality a symbol of original sin.

Today we don't ask permission to eat an

apple or drink apple juice, as in the story of the
Celtic poet, Ken. He persuaded the lords of the air to
let him pick just one more apple. Then he was able
to cling to the tree so tightly that he couldn't be
pulled away. In this way he protected his poetic
immortality. For the saying goes that anyone who
manages to suck the juice from an apple, while

clinging to the apple tree in stormy weather, is too sinful to go to heaven, but is safe from hell.

The Celts had only two fruit trees in their calendar: the fig and the apple. Both must have meant a great deal to them. They stand either side of the summer and winter solstices. They do not occupy these positions because their leaves, flowers or fruit are particularly distinctive at that time. Indeed, they bloom in May and June, and their fruit ripens in September.

The Celts were probably more impressed by the beautiful five-pointed star in the heart of the fruit. You can see it when you cut an apple in two across the middle rather than lengthways. For them five was the number of love, and above all they loved what they called the 'Other World' into which they could be initiated by the birch.

You must understand eternity before you can earn it. When an apple tree dies, it can say: it is finished. It is the tree of fulfilment that follows the birch, the tree of initiation.

The Celts said that people who were born in summer between 25 June and 4 July, and in winter between 23 December and 1 January, were the link connecting all that is separate. They are intermediaries between heaven and earth, between the ideal and reality, and between good and evil.

They never let themselves get dragged so far into the swamp of life that they get bogged down. They never long so much for the 'heavenly' ideal that they despise earthly existence. Their model is love of life as a whole. They follow their natural mood swings and bend sometimes towards one extreme, sometimes to the other. They do not see feeling and reason as contradictory. Like two lovers, they either agree or disagree, depending on the situation.

Their moral tolerance is exemplary. They seem to accept that everyone should answer to his own conscience for his own way of living. Rejecting unrealisable dogmas, however worthwhile they seem, they prefer to practise the art of the possible and, as far as they can, to moderate extreme lifestyles and value judgements.

Perhaps this is why those born during the days of the apple prefer to surround themselves with people they can help, rather than the other way round. They often find themselves in a dilemma over security and independence, and usually opt for independence without outside help. In this they resemble their tree of life.

All apple trees are extremely robust and will grow in almost any type of soil. And people who were born during the days of the apple have let themselves be grafted onto a thousand different tasks in the service of man's development, just as over a thousand types of apple have been developed through grafting. In spite of their moodiness they are really the most balanced of people in their attitude to life. 'Apple trees' seldom abandon themselves to passive world-weariness. They can always find someone who suffers more than they do, and in helping these people they pull themselves out of their depression. They manage to reconcile their use of power with their longing for unity.

Natives of the apple: Rudyard Kipling, Henry Miller, Marlene Dietrich, Mao Tse-Tung.
Gem stone: The tourmaline, of any colour, which protects against deception.
Number: 36.
Medicinal use: An apple a day keeps the doctor away.
Motto: He who is grateful does not expect gratitude.

THE FIR
guardian of all births

Fir is the poetic name for the spruce (*Picea*), of which there are about 50 different species, all very similar in appearance. Fir is also the name given to the type of conifer called *Abies*. This genus too consists of about 50 species. Both are called fir by the layman. Most grow so readily and so tall and straight that they are among the tallest trees of Europe. At 80 or 120 years old a fir tree measures a good 60 metres (200 feet).

The Celts saw true greatness in their independent spirit. Firs choose the most inhospitable places on shaded alpine slopes. In high mountain regions they cling to the rocks with their strong but shallow roots, bathe in the clouds and let their own needles fall to provide themselves with the tiny amount of soil they need.

In the lowlands the old firs, standing alone with their sweeping branches curving upwards at the tip, appear like massive brooding hens. While they are small silver firs depend on the shade of their mother trees; too much light does them no good. Norway spruces are less fussy. Like well-behaved children they grow in serried ranks wherever they have been planted. Deer nibble at them, but not at the silver fir. They grow quickly. After a couple of years they are sold as Christmas trees, after 15 years as wood for fencing and after 70 to 80 years as building timber.

Stradivari, Amati, Bergonzi and other famous violin-makers climbed high into the mountains and spent days at a time sounding out spruce trunks from top to bottom with their own hands. Only a fir that has grown slowly provides the ideal wood for the tone required. In places where the soil is almost barren and the winters are long, everything grows slowly, which improves the quality.

Anyone wandering through a pine wood for the first time is strangely impressed. Light can scarcely penetrate the tree cover. Hardly a ray reaches the bare, impoverished soil. When the wind blows through them it booms like dangerous breakers, and in a storm you can hear the crash of dead branches falling or the unintelligible moaning and groaning of branches rubbing against each other. Old pine woods have a magical effect, magical like a primeval mother, magical as birth.

Perhaps this was why the fir replaced the yew during the period from 2 to 11 January. It is cold and gloomy then, and the evergreen fir trees are a welcome sight. They are taken as a promise that life will

return, as a symbol of the victory of life over death.

But the days of the fir also occur between 5 and 14 July. At that time of the year new, light-green life has burst out from all the branches and twigs and clothed the high mountain firs in their most cheerful apparel.

People who were born during the days of the fir are very reserved in their personal affairs. They know they are vulnerable and go to great lengths to blend in with their surroundings. They hide behind a protective mask of conventions, principles and much more. What lengths would a person go to in order to feel safe? When 'firs' finally find the confidence to take off their protective mask, they are the most reliable of friends. The impregnable defences which could be sensed around them are then transformed into a garden in which all feelings thrive as they should.

In his autobiographical novel *A la recherche du temps perdu*, (*In Search of Time Past*), Marcel Proust

describes various ways in which those who were born during the days of the fir try to be both safe and free. Simone de Beauvoir, however, lived and worked on the fir's theme of life in quite a different way. Everyone should read her book *La Vieillesse*, (*Old Age*) while they are young. It teaches us to have fewer illusions about the security that life has to offer and so shows us how to be a good mother to ourselves. That is the surest way to achieve security. Anyone who cannot find an unshakeable primeval confidence in life deep within himself, tends to fall between two stools, most of all in his relationships. If fir people demand their partner's support to the exclusion of all else, if they are afraid of being alone, then they will remain dependent on them. This is beneath the dignity of a hardy mountain pine.

Those who demand safety and security from the world receive the opposite. It is better to give the world what it does not have to offer. So every birth brings a little more light into the mysterious darkness, like the fir tree at Christmas.

In the chapter on the yew you can read how the fir drove it out of this place which it originally occupied.

Natives of the fir: Marcel Proust, Simone de Beauvoir, Friedrich Dürrenmatt.

Gem stone: Amber, which was the first gem stone.
Number: 18.
Medicinal use: Chewing the resin of the fir protects against shrinking gums.
Motto: Everything hard is born of softness, everything big is born of smallness.

THE ELM
the good-tempered tree

About 12,000 years ago, after the last ice age, the elm and the oak returned together to central and northern Europe. They did not form woods, but light and airy groves. Later, as Europe became Christianised, men ceased to care for them and they were replaced by massive dark beech woods.

Today, after millions of years of evolution, the resistance of the elms seems to have been broken and they are threatened with extinction. Ninety per cent of the stock in Central Europe has been infected with what is known as Dutch elm disease, to which elms have been succumbing in increasing numbers since the 1920s. It has three causes, all equally culpable: the fungus *Ceratocystis ulmi*, the elm bark beetle, and man, who has dug channels to divert all the rain water into the rivers as quickly as possible and is thus responsible for the drastic fall in the level of the water table.

There are now only about 20 types of elm in the temperate northern latitudes, mostly huge trees. They are frequently identified wrongly because they have the same massive trunk with a great variety of

forms and the same large leaves as the lime tree, and
the shape of the branches and the fanlike arrangement of the twigs and leaves resembles that of the
beech. Many 'village lime trees' are elms, and many
'lime tree avenues' should be called elm avenues.
Elms never form woods, but they are distinctive for
the wonderful structure of their branches, which are
very regularly distributed and develop an almost
uniform thickness. They sweep upwards in beautiful
curves, then their tips curve down, like a fountain
with four spouts.

Elms can be divided into four groups: cork
elms, field elms, mountain elms and fluttering elms.

Cork elms are striking because of their
straight, stiff habit. Their branches are only slightly
curved, their leaves only half as big as those of the
field elms. The furrowed corky bark is brown in
colour. After a few years it cracks and splits like the
bark of an old tree, the trunk full of warts and
bumps. They are hardly ever propagated by seed,
but more usually by suckers from the roots, which
are useful for hedging. The roots, just below the surface in damp ground, send hundreds of little shoots
springing up towards the light.

Field elms are drawn towards the south.
They are even to be found in North Africa, but
only, as in Europe and the Near East, along the

lowland riverbanks. In damp ground they grow to a height of 30 metres (100 feet). The leaves are remarkable, of a green that defies description. They are narrow, not stiff and less rough than the leaves of other elms. The twigs are thin and shiny, the buds dull and black. There are short cracks in the bark. This type of elm is propagated by both seeds and root suckers.

Although the mountain elm has more or less overcome its fear of the mountains, it is still hardly typical of mountain trees. It never grows above middle height and chooses protected locations between the rocks where it is shady and the soil is damp. Like all elms its root system is shallow and it is thus susceptible to being blown over by the wind. Its foliage is always quite sparse, but its leaves are big, up to 15 centimetres (six inches) long, so that the tree appears to be fully covered. The leaves have a very short stalk and are almost round, thin and very rough. Its dark green, spreading crown looks beautiful with its strong, hairy, dark brown twigs. This elm in particular propagates itself by far-flying seeds, but hardly ever from suckers.

The fluttering elm is so called because it forms loose bunches of long-stalked, round, 'fluttering' winged seeds. Most stay in the valleys. Their thin, light-brown twigs are full of hairy one-year-old shoots. In old age the bark is grey and peels off in flat, thin strips, something which does not happen to any other kind of elm. Like the cork elm, the fluttering elm prefers swampy ground to dry ground, if given the choice.

It is also worth mentioning the ornamental garden forms: the weeping elm and the pyramid elm. The branches of the first sweep down, giving it an umbrella-shaped crown. It is the most attractive weeping tree apart from the weeping willow. In the pyramid elm the branches are upright, forming a pyramidal or cone-shaped crown. This type of elm is the preferred choice for street planting.

All types of elm give the impression of coming into leaf twice over. The flowers, which appear in abundance, often as early as March, look like young leaves. These then lose their colour at the end of April and make way for the real leaves. In dry years these may fall as early as August, particularly if the ground is sandy or stony. In good, damp soil they remain magnificently green until the middle of October and do not fall until the end of the month, when they have hardly turned yellow.

Elm wood grows twice as fast as oak and apart from the wood of the fluttering elm which is soft and white, is as hard and as durable as oak. Although it is very difficult to split and work, it is still used in the construction of furniture. The wood was also formerly used by wood turners and coach-builders, in ship-building and in hydraulic engineering. Beautifully grained pipe bowls were often made from elm wood, and these attracted the attention of cabinet-makers.

The elm occupies the periods from 12 to 24 January and from 15 to 25 July. The Celts must have noticed the correspondence between the elm's rapid growth into a beautiful, regular form and the beautiful, regular increase and decrease in the daylight. For them the days of the elm were times when they felt well disposed towards their fellow men. In the cold of winter there was little else for them to do, and in July this bonhomie was induced by the warmth and richness of nature.

Elms tolerate a great deal. If you were born between 12 and 24 January or between 15 and 25

July, then tolerance and fairness are your model and the socially orientated individual your ideal. There is no contradiction, as far as you are concerned, in living your own life and at the same time responding to a fundamental feeling of solidarity with your fellow men. It is only a contradiction for people who confuse egotism with individuality. Such people do not like you, whilst people who run with the pack, that is those who hide behind the clichés of the majority and abuse generally accepted morals for their own egotism, like you even less.

At first you believe that all people are individualists and as fair, generous and ready to help as you are. The word 'in-dividual' originally meant 'the undivided indivisible', in the sense of 'love your neighbour as yourself'. But unfortunately it has now become completely alienated from its original meaning, and in many places an individualist is regarded as odd, eccentric, even an outsider. Don't people often laugh at you, just because you don't conform to stereotypes or because you don't dress according to fashion? When it comes to giving practical help they look the other way. In this world of mutual suspicion and restriction you suddenly become an outsider because of your equitable disposition and natural helpfulness. Your courage in going your own way, encouraging the unusual and finding pleasure in the unfamiliar, exasperates those who behave like sheep, simply because they aren't brave enough to follow your example.

You are probably quite unaware of the value of your ability to conquer anxiety, just as you are unaware that you are hard-working, reliable and creative. You don't try to belong to any group and you don't want to be organised. On the contrary, you are allergic to labels, even respectable ones. You are overcome by embarrassment when the spotlight falls on you. Your sense of moderation alerts you to the fact that an excess of light for one person can soon become too little for someone else. You would rather hide your own light under a bushel than take it away from anyone else. You prefer to praise your fellow men than to be exposed to their praise.

How do all those people who were born during the days of the elm, but who cannot express themselves creatively, actually cope with the widespread lack of principle in this world? They console themselves with the world of fantasy, where they can make a gâteau from a piece of bread, a hero from a 'misery' of a partner and a dream palace from a crummy, noisy flat. The truth is what we internalise our experiences. Most of the time external appearances are deceptive!

Natives of the elm: Albert Schweitzer, Alexandre Dumas, Molière, Patricia Highsmith.

Gem stone: The moonstone, which makes people gentle and compassionate.

Number: 14.

Medicinal use: Tea made with the leaves of the elm relieves diarrhoea.

Motto: What we do for others, we also do for ourselves.

THE CYPRESS
the tree of resurrection

Cypresses (*Cupressus*) belong to that large family of conifers which already existed a hundred million years before the first deciduous trees.

The diverse group of cypress plants is impressively large. It includes eighteen types, spread throughout the northern and southern hemispheres. They are slow-growing trees of medium height which live for a long time. Their wood is usually hard and above all smells good. For this reason the American colonists called many of the cypresses there cedars—for example, the Californian or Chilean river cedar.

Besides these 'false cedars' which are actually cypresses, there are many kinds of 'false cypress', including the dwarf cypress which grows to a height of 60 metres (200 feet). No other kind reaches this height, yet this is the one referred to as the 'dwarf'. Tree names are as illogical as language itself, whose roots also lie in the darkness of the past.

We are concerned here with the true cypresses. They differ from the false cypresses in that their bushy branches stick out in all directions,

their woody cones are usually larger and stronger, and the cross-section of their shoots is round or angular. Half the 20 different species of real cypress grow in small groves in California. Five more grow in Arizona and Mexico. A particularly undemanding species has even chosen the Sahara Desert as its home. The Romans in North Africa cultivated it, prizing its scented, beautifully grained 'lemon wood'. Another kind, the 'Kashmir cypress', yearns for its home in Tibet. It is a rare blue-green tree which is not as winter hardy as its homeland would seem to imply.

Apart from the false cypresses, the best known of all is the Italian cypress (*Cupressus semper-virens*), an elegant, columnar, evergreen tree. Originally it had a broad crown, but in ancient times it developed its present form through selective breeding. In general, where it grows wild it gives the impression of a landscape developed by man. In northern Europe it thrives only in protected locations, but it does better in England and Scotland where the winters are milder.

The Gowens cypress, named after the Scottish horticulturist J. Gowen, is characterised by reddish-brown cones which occur in bunches on the previous year's shoots. Beside this modest wild plant, which comes from California, the Arizona cypress grows into an impressive tree 15 metres (50 feet) high. In northern Europe it is almost winter hardy, tolerates most sites and a great deal of rain. The death of other types of cypress in Tuscany led to its introduction there. Today it tolerates the climatic fluctuations that occur there better than the indigenous cypresses.

Not surprisingly, there are impressive specimens in Ireland of a type of cypress which has large cones and massive branches set low down, which make the tree appear as broad as it is high. Like the Highlands of Scotland, Ireland was not conquered and much of the Celtic cultural heritage has been preserved. This includes a love of the tree of resurrection.

Nor is it surprising that this light- and sun-hungry tree should attract such attention between 25 January and 3 February, and between 26 July and 4 August. At the end of January and the beginning of February the days are at last getting longer, and although the 'light curve' does not rise quite so sharply as it falls in August, the sunlight is experienced just as intensely.

Just like the tree, those born during the days of the cypress seem to have a particular need for plenty of light and sunshine, and are correspondingly affected by a lack of sunlight. Traditionally,

human qualities such as striving for the clarity of autonomy are associated with sun and light. A high percentage of people who are self-employed, or who busy themselves as they choose in the interests of a cause, an idea, their fellow men or, in exceptional cases, themselves, must belong to those who were born during the days of the cypress. To be hungry for light also means to battle for recognition or even to be willing to sacrifice one's last shirt for freedom. In any event, it is difficult to find a 'cypress person' who doesn't stand out, both for his buoyant sense of purpose and his equally ebullient happiness.

Those who were born during the days of the cypress are able to bear terrible misfortunes calmly and to learn from them how to find the way to freedom from sorrow and worldly troubles. Many succeed in holding their own individual line between highly praised positive thinking and proscribed negative thinking, or finding it again relatively quickly. Biting irony or sarcasm loaded with reality, even directed against themselves, are the product of these endeavours.

Natives of the cypress: Wolfgang Amadeus Mozart, George Bernard Shaw, James Joyce, George Orwell, Aldous Huxley, Jacqueline Onassis.

Gem stone: Tanzanite, which helps to maintain independence.

Number: 8.

Medicinal use: The scent of crumbled cypress leaves increases concentration.

Motto: He who would be free must free himself from the demand for freedom.

THE CEDAR
the tree of nobility

Amongst the conifers there is no tree that can compare with the majestic shape of the cedar (*Cedrus*).

Many tree experts will wonder why the cedar is included in this ancient tree calendar. It is probably the most often-mentioned tree in the Bible, but the first Cedar of Lebanon didn't reach Europe until 1646, when it was planted in the garden of the vicarage of Childrey in the Thames Valley. The Atlantic cedar from Morocco reached our latitudes for the first time in 1839, the Cyprus cedar and the Himalayan cedar not until this century.

But if we bear in mind that, over the centuries, the Celts maintained contact with all the settlements they had founded, it becomes clear that the cedar was as well known to Celtic peoples as any other tree today. Many place names remind us just how far Celtic culture spread, from Russia in the east to Portugal in the west, from Galatia in Asia Minor to the far north of Scotland.

Anyone who has seen and smelt the natural cedar forests which have been preserved up to the present day in the Taurus Mountains of the south-

east of Turkey, or in Lebanon, will not forget them for as long as they live. About 400 of these giant trees survive on the slopes of the mountains of Lebanon, at a height of 1,200 to 1,800 metres (4,000 to 6,000 feet) above sea level. The largest there has a circumference of 15 metres (50 feet), reaches a height of 40 metres (132 feet) and is estimated to be 2,500 years old.

The beautiful, sweet-smelling, durable and

versatile wood of the cedar of Lebanon, and probably that of the Atlantic cedar as well, was the most
important wood in the Mediterranean region in
ancient times. Although it grows fast—to a height of
15 metres (50 feet) in 30 years, and up to 40 metres
(132 feet) in 150 years—this indispensable species of
tree has almost been wiped out. At the end of the
seventeenth century John Evelyn tried to rescue it.
But it couldn't be planted in Europe in large numbers until the first trees began to produce cones.

Cedars are propagated by seed and need a
really mild climate. They became very fashionable in
the middle of the eighteenth century when the Duke
of Richmond had a thousand of them planted at
Goodwood.

The Atlantic cedar from North Africa is very
similar. It grows more upright, and appears to be a
little slimmer because the tips of its branches soar up
rather than spreading out horizontally like those of
the cedar of Lebanon. It is a little less sensitive to the
cold and grows better in alkaline soil than its rela-
tives. Its wood is of the same quality as that of the
cedar of Lebanon.

The Himalayan cedar, a somewhat taller tree
at 60 metres (197 feet), which grows in the western
Himalayas and in Afghanistan up to 3,000 metres
(10,000 feet) above sea level, is rich in resin and is the

most intensely perfumed—like cedarwood oil. It grows into a slender, conical tree, and appears graceful rather than majestic with its branches hanging down. In its youth it is the most tender of all the cedars and does not always survive the winter in Central Europe.

The fourth true cedar comes from Cyprus. It grows slowly and then only to half the height of the cedar of Lebanon. Everything about it is modest. It is called *Cedrus brevifolia*. Like all the cedars, it doesn't bloom until autumn.

People who were born during the days of the cedar, from 14 to 23 August and from 9 to 18 February, don't waste time thinking about inspiration, but live an inspired life instead. Watchful and reflective, they aim to fulfil their 'destiny'. They assume a leading role, not because they are at all missionary-minded, but because they are under an obligation from a clear inner voice. In this way, whether they succeed or fail, they preserve their equanimity or at least their clear approach. The fact that they are serving not just themselves, but above all their mission, gives them strength and confidence and frequently lends them an aura of nobility.

This is also true of modest 'Cyprus cedars' who put their heart and soul into things and achieve a great deal for themselves and their surroundings, both internally and externally. 'Clever on the outside and nothing on the inside' bears as little relationship to those born during the days of the cedar as does the opposite. They are marked out by their efforts to find agreement between thinking and behaviour, between reason and feeling, between personal autonomy and supra-personal interrelationships through serving others.

Natives of the cedar: Abraham Lincoln, Napoleon I, Louis XVI, Menachem Begin, Boris Pasternak.
Gem stone: The topaz, of whatever colour, which brings moderation to existence.
Number: 1.
Medicinal use: Chewing the resin of the cedar gives self-confidence.
Motto: If you want to make the world a better place, better yourself and you will then have bettered the world.

THE PINE
mother of wisdom

The pine (*Pinus*), a modest, but pioneering tree, is the most frequently planted of all the pine family. Its spread throughout the northern hemisphere, from the Arctic Circle to the Equator, is not just natural. Since it makes no particular demands about type of soil or climate, it has been introduced in places where other useful timber trees would fail to thrive. It grows on rocks and in sparse sandy soil. It is not particularly bothered by either icy winds or burning sun. It is prepared for all that.

As a tree which relies on the wind to distribute its seeds the pine values every kind of wind there is. So it does not brace itself against the wind. On the contrary. It offers its crown to the wind and the light. It doesn't grow in the shape of a candle, wrapped round by protecting branches, like the fir and the spruce. It forms what could be described as 'open floors', spreading out its crown in the shape of an umbrella like a deciduous tree. Its graceful beauty has made it a favourite with garden designers, above all in Japan.

It should be clear that we are dealing here with the common pine (*Pinus sylvestris*), although it has received other names, depending on the location, and has acquired a host of variations that would fill a whole book. The Swiss and the British call it 'Scots pine', while in the Mediterranean they give the name 'pine' to every kind of pine, including the Scots pine which is the only North-European pine to have survived the last ice age.

Over ten thousand years ago almost the whole of Europe was covered by vast primeval forests of pine and birch. They were the first trees to move back into the regions freed from the ice, and they prepared the soil for the slow advance of the great deciduous trees, which since then have nearly driven out the pines.

The pine was well-known to the Celts as the 'fire tree'. Our ancestors lit their homes with pinewood spills from pine trees. With the resin of the *kienforhas* they made torches to guide them through the darkness of the night. Just as the dog is the loyal servant of man, so the pine tree is the loyal servant of trees. It goes first, searching out and preparing the soil for others to survive in.

In North America a species of pine has received a reward commensurate with its inestimable service. Specimens of *Pinus Longaeva*, which grows there, are among the oldest living beings on the earth – 5,000 years young! Waste not, want not!

It is hard to save in a time of abundance. In the days of the pine, from 24 August to 2 September, cautious people think about bringing in the harvest, sharing it out and storing it. And during the other pine days, 19–29 February, they harvest the fruits of their foresight. The abundance of harvest time should cater for the shortfall experienced in early spring.

Can you wonder that people who were born into an atmosphere like this have to be careful, far-seeing, cautious and hard-working? Anyone who wants to take such precautions must always do more than appears necessary at the time. Those who bring in the harvest need self-control and common sense, otherwise there will soon be nothing left.

The supply of unlimited amounts of daylight comes to an end every year at the end of August. At that time pine tree people light the lamp of good sense, and in early spring the light of hope. But their hope is hardly ever restricted to passive waiting, it is the clever exploitation of age-old experience. Clever forethought and reflection.

Just as their tree of life forms quiet woods in which each tree keeps a reasonable distance from those next to it, so pine tree natives take as much interest in themselves as they do in their community. They have good grounds for fearing those so-called altruists who always want to help so that they themselves will receive even more help. That is, they bring a great deal of muddle into the life of the community, and confusion of instincts and feelings makes pine tree people uneasy, just as wet ground holds little appeal for the real pine tree.

On the other hand they are far too intelligent to behave egotistically. An advantage for a 'pine tree' always turns out to be an advantage for their partner too.

'Pine trees' are not theoreticians, they are above all practitioners of life. At the very least they take the trouble to thoroughly test their theory of living. They let no one take up the time they have put aside for that.

Many people look for occupations in which they are allowed to enjoy, at the same time, order and mood, self-control and self-intoxication. How big or small a wheel is in the water of life is irrelevant. The main thing is that they make a contribution which brings happiness to the world. While it is small and weak, it needs security and regularity. That is why foresight is the mother of wisdom.

If we take the pine tree as our model, then healthy moderation will return to our life.

Natives of the pine: Victor Hugo, Johann Wolfgang von Goethe, Leonard Bernstein, Ingrid Bergman.
Gem stone: Rock crystal, which encourages real modesty.
Number: 15.
Medicinal use: The steam from boiled pine shoots helps to ease coughs and hoarseness.
Motto: A longing for perfection is an illness, which is cured with conciliation.

THE WILLOW
a many-sided citizen of the world

A speciality of the willow (*Salix*) is its coloured bark. Many shrub and tree forms have colourful young shoots: red, yellow, green, orange, white, crimson or brown.

The genus includes about 300 species which have spread over the whole of the northern hemisphere and as far as South America and South Africa. Because willows are frequently hybridised it is very difficult to tell the different species apart. Under certain circumstances a prostrate dwarf form can even cross-pollinate with a magnificent large tree. Therefore many hybrid forms occur, of which the bush types are more successful.

Even though it is difficult to tell the species apart, it is much easier to determine the sex of a willow. Willows are not self-fertile. Each individual plant produces either the mainly silvery-green female catkins or the yellow male anthers. The seeds of the willow are white, covered with tiny white hairs which enable them to fly far and wide.

Willows, however, can be propagated by cuttings even more easily than the poplar. It was an Englishman who first described how readily they

rooted. At the beginning of the eighteenth century
he brought home from China a package tied up with
willow wands. Carelessly, he threw the 'ties' into a
corner of his garden. The first weeping willows in
Europe grew from these. It is in any case certain that
the weeping willow comes from western China and
not, as its Latin name *Salix babylonica* would suggest,
from the Middle East.

Today it is our most popular ornamental tree
in parks with ponds, on river banks or lakesides. It
seems to stretch out its branches to the water, but in
fact it does this to catch the light reflected from the
water. It receives an ample water supply from the
soil, thanks to its thick root system. Because it
spreads so quickly and weaves its roots through the
soil in all directions, we plant willows to strengthen
the embankments of streams, rivers and roads.

The place of the willow in the Celtic tree calendar is determined by reference to a simple, natural
fact: in autumn, from 3 to 12 September, the willow
stems are full of sap. This is the best time to cut them,
for they will then remain supple enough to weave for
a much longer time. And this is harvest time, when the
basket, woven out of willow wands, is king.

The willow uses the first ten days of the first
month of spring, from 1 to 10 March, to open its
flowers, regardless of what the weather may do. The

tree is under the sway of the moon goddess who
watches over birth and death on earth. In the Middle
Ages it was regarded as the tree of witches, who flew
on broomsticks made of willow twigs.

If you were born during the days of the willow tree (1–10 March and 3–12 September) the willow will be your tree of life. It doesn't necessarily
have to be a weeping willow. You can choose any
type of willow you like: none of them is alien to you.
Mentally, and often spiritually, you are as flexible as
a willow wand. You dare to sit at the same table as
the beggar and the king, the angels and the devils.

Your tolerance, which has its roots in your
deep experience of humanity, enables you to
empathise with very varied and also difficult people.
Only dry-as-dust technocrats leave a bitter taste in
your mouth. You are as dependent on lively feelings
as your tree of life is on water.

After the great Chinese poet Lao Tse had spent some time sleeping under a weeping willow, he said: 'Who knows whether we dream during our life or live in a dream.' Doesn't this correspond with your moods? Don't dreams play a bigger part in your life than razor-sharp reason? The answer is not important. The question itself contains the answer. With their practical, intuitive nature 'willow trees' are frequently to be found where they can fulfil mankind's dreams.

Everyone has good and bad habits. But 'willow trees' don't seem to be bound by them. They switch from the most unusual to the merely mundane as if there were no difference between them. While others go grey on the treadmill of everyday life, they remain unruffled. In the most hectic rush they appear quiet, like deep water.

People of this type cannot be pinned down. Hardly have they taken up the cudgels on behalf of a conservative cause than they are entertaining us with extremely progressive ideas. They insist on certainty and take the biggest risks. Trifles break their hearts and they take great misfortunes quite admirably in their stride. They understand everything except themselves. They are simply related to the willow, they grow tall in a flash. In a favourable site some kinds can grow to a good 20 metres (65 feet) in 15 years, with a circumference of one and a half metres (five feet). Then they are cut down. Shortly after that the young shoots burst out of the mother stump again. Willows and willow natives accept life and death and are therefore probably the favourite guests of nature. In any event, they usually have almost miraculous luck in their fight against the elements on the sea, in the air and on the earth. Others say that they must have a good, deep relationship with their guardian angel. But Mother Earth is ready to protect all her children so long as they don't oppose her. This idea would never occur to 'willow trees'. On the contrary, they make themselves subservient to the earth which they are happy to serve. Those who protect life are protected by life!

Natives of the willow: Alexander Graham Bell, Joseph Niepce, Ferdinand Porsche, Yuri Gagarin.
Gem stone: Precious beryl, which makes people attentive.
Number: 10.
Medicinal use: Tea made from willow bark lowers any fever, even the fever of love.
Motto: While we are living one life, we are already dreaming of the next.

THE LIME
the nurse of the oak

Everything about the lime tree (*Tilia*) is gentle, meaning flexible, smooth and agile, and yet every type has its vices!

The nurses of great men and women do not come down in the annals of history. They do their duty and go. Wrangling over ranks and names is not in their nature. The lime tree, in the shelter of which the hard oak is planted, was already a favourite with people in bygone ages although felling a lime tree was not punishable by law. Today, in certain circumstances, it would arouse indignation and protest.

The lime tree has withstood every change of power, from the Celts to the Romans, from the Romans to the Christians, and from feudalism to democracy. Beneath it Siegfried killed the dragon Fafnir. As he was bathing in the dragon's blood in order to attain immortality, the lime tree let a leaf fall between his shoulderblades. As a result of this his heart remained vulnerable. Hagen, his adversary, killed him under a lime tree.

Whenever people needed to find the truth in legal wrangling, they met under an old lime tree. For beneath it the real truth comes to light, its perfume puts the judge in a clement mood and the disputing parties reach an amicable agreement.

In the Middle Ages the wood of the lime was called holy wood, *lignum sanctum*. Many world-famous saints have been carved from this wood. Today it is used for brush handles, for making drawing boards and other articles that have to be light.

The wood is still highly thought of, and so is the tea made from the flowers of the lime. These must be picked fresh each year, because after a year they lose the healing power that treats every kind of cold and chill. But don't throw the old lime flowers away. Sew them into little linen sachets and hide them here and there. They will protect you from actions which are prompted by passion!

The summer lime and the rather smaller winter lime are the only native species in Central Europe. The Dutch lime is the result of the spontaneous hybridisation of these two. It grows up to 45 metres (148 feet). Suckers from the roots which compete with the main trunk are a problem. If they are shortened the trees form thick bearded stumps. If they are cut out the trees grow to twice the size, like dragon's heads.

All limes, including the cultivated kinds, as, for example, the 'upright Swedish lime' and the

silver lime which gleams and sparkles silver in the moonlight, are regularly attacked by aphids. They cover the leaves and twigs with sugar sap. This honeydew attracts the honeydew fungus. The stickiness drips down and turns the leaves black. The positive side of this drawback is that they teem with ladybirds.

Only the Crimean lime is resistant to aphids. Its perfume draws bees to it irresistibly. Dazed or even poisoned by its nectar, they fall to the ground. The ground is littered with dying creatures. The heart-shaped leaves gleam innocently in the sunshine.

The search for a lime tree with no drawbacks will go on, even though the *Tilia oliveri* from China has been growing in Europe since 1900. With its upright growth, open crown, smooth grey branches and large flat leaves it is perfect—and hardly ever planted.

Those who were born during the days of the lime tree, from 11 to 20 March and from 13 to 22 September, happily put up with whatever life brings them. No doubt they say, 'Everything is all right as it is', and yet they still ask: 'Why are my ideas and dreams always much better than reality?' Schubert's *lied* of the lime tree standing by the fountain in front of the gate gives one of the most beautiful answers. And in the tree circle, too, the lime tree stands at the beginning of the new spring, at the beginning of autumn, at the equinoxes.

It is found in the region which is not of this world. Only in this way can it take on and fulfil the role of nurse. Are not our ideas, desires and dreams the nurses of our lives? What is there that is beautiful in our life that was not first a dream?

Natives of the lime are particularly susceptible to signals from the world where everything is perfect. Some succeed in letting at least a small part of this perfection leave its mark on life on this earth. Let us forgive them for daring to look at the world through the rose-tinted spectacles of their dreams and imaginings and for often coming to grief on the eternal sameness of grey, everyday life, either because they take it too seriously or because they are floating above it. Without them we would often not know how beautiful things can be. We would forget that passion and imperfection exist. But thanks to the lime tree even our heart remains vulnerable!

Natives of the lime tree: Henrik Ibsen, Albert Einstein, Greta Garbo, Agatha Christie.
Gem stone: Pearls, which strengthen passion.
Number: 12.
Medicinal use: Finely powdered lime charcoal purifies and disinfects the gums, among other things.
Motto: The pain of life is the price one pays for the pleasure of life.

THE OLIVE
the tree that lives wisely

The olive tree (*Olea*) can live for 1,500 to 2,000 years. Apart from the yew it is the longest lived tree in Europe.

'Where the grape ripens, where the almond flowers, where the black-brown eyes of the girls glow, where the snowflake never falls, there, to the land of the olive tree, let us go!' So said Orgetorix, and plunged the iron sword into his heart to prove that it was not a desire for power that had induced him to lead the Helvetii to the south.

The olive is a stocky tree, growing to a height of 12 metres (40 feet), and full of grace and dignity. Its densely-packed branches spread out just above the ground and weave their way upwards, where they bear blue-green leaves that gleam silver on the underside. Its wood is hard, compact, finely grained and eminently suitable for carving and turning on the lathe. For hundreds of years olive wood has been used to make plates, bowls and cutlery, and also clubs. But it is the healthy, oil-rich fruit which has made it, along with the fig tree and the grape vine, a symbol of happiness and prosperity. The olive tree also teaches us the secrets of well-being: modest demands, the ability to withstand transplanting and a lot of light. It needs well aerated soil. A third of it should be sand so that water drains through it quickly. Wetness is the greatest enemy of the olive. It grows slowly, but if its roots are carefully dug out of the ground and equally carefully dug in again, even very old trees can be successfully transplanted.

The olive tree is an extremely 'heliophile' plant. That means that the sun is its friend, and it needs a great deal of sunlight. But in our part of the world it can also be grown in a light room where the dry air corresponds to the conditions in its homeland.

When you next eat black olives—the green ones are simply unripe—do not throw the stones away. Plant them in light, sandy soil two centimetres (one inch) deep. The seeds will germinate in four to six weeks, but it may take two to three months. So don't lose patience.

Olives can also be propagated by means of cuttings. From April to May cut the tips of shoots about 20 centimetres (eight inches) long, put them into damp sand to a depth of half their length, place a plastic cover over them and put them in a shady place. Two to three months later they will have rooted. Then the cuttings can be carefully trans-

planted to light, sandy soil and just as carefully accustomed to the sun.

The day of the olive tree is 23 September, the day of the autumn equinox. Light and darkness are absolutely equal. In the tree circle the olive tree stands exactly opposite the oak. What starts in spring as the primeval life force achieves fulfilment

in autumn as the wisdom of life. Naturally, that doesn't mean that everyone who celebrates their birthday on 23 September is clever and wise. The characteristic of this day is much more effective as a role model. Anyone who is able to live up to it is always remembered in the most positive way.

They work to ensure harmony, justice and beauty both on a personal level and in broader contexts. They serve the community admirably. They frequently undertake tasks which no one else wants to take on, without any trace of self-interest. Nothing is too trivial for them, nothing too difficult, if it means they can contribute something to the welfare of their fellow men.

The two most striking examples of the essence of those who were born on the day of the olive tree are to be found at the beginning and the end of the Roman Empire. The one at the beginning is a man, the one at the end a woman. We all know about the man. Everyone has heard of the first Roman Emperor, Augustus. But historians have, almost to a man, kept quiet about the woman, whilst history teachers have ignored her completely. Have you ever heard of the Roman Empress, Galla Placidia? What this woman achieved, 1,500 years ago, for peace and understanding in Europe could be a model for solving the problems of our modern era. A great deal could be learnt from her story by anyone who is interested in studying human nature.

The sensitive adaptability of those born under the sign of the olive is actually dangerous for them in an insensitive world which profanes everything. They easily get dragged down into what is fashionable. They do too much to keep the peace in the hope that the extra effort will help their ideal. They become victims of mass taste, victims of their time.

This is why it is important for everyone, and especially for olive natives, to rise above their time, to look at the past, the present and the future as one great big whole; to let sense, feeling and reason work together simultaneously as equal partners. Wisdom cannot be expressed in words any more than truth can. It is an experience, something to be lived through, and a deeply-held feeling that everything is good just as it is.

Natives of the olive: Ray Charles, Romy Schneider.
Gem stone: The diamond, which changes the darkness into light.
Number: 6.
Medicinal use: Cold-pressed olive oil helps psoriasis.
Motto: Self-assertion strengthens.

THE YEW
the outcast tree of death

The question that springs to mind with regard to the yew (*Taxus*) is: Why was it displaced in the tree calendar? Apart from the oak, the yew must have enjoyed the highest prestige in the eyes of the Celts. The druids always stressed that every Celt was descended from the god of death. Just like the Samurai in Japan who committed suicide if they could not achieve a particular goal, the Celtic warriors fell on their swords, often just to give more weight to an idea.

But after the Romans had systematically wiped out the druids, belief in reincarnation disappeared along with their culture. The gloomy yew forests, which the Romans hardly dared enter, were cut down and cleared away. Fast-growing spruces took their place. Only birth was regarded as a happy event. Death was given a sting which it did not deserve.

Taxus baccata is the Latin name of this strange tree, which nowadays is incapable of forming woods without human help. It may be a conifer, but it is not a self-fertile plant. It needs a neighbour of the other sex in order to set seed. Propagation is also made more difficult because of its slow growth. The yew keeps its stocky shape right into old age. The bumpy, gnarled trunk, which shows deep, irregular, at times almost angular grooves, is barely visible. It envelops itself from the ground upwards in ever darker green garb. Its branches, which at first grow horizontally and then strain steeply upwards, can be pruned as needed. They grow back again so there is always greenery on the trunk. Although in its youth its luxuriant growth forms the shape of a spindle, it develops an irregular network of branches, which grow close together. Only small animals are able to climb them.

Yews can be trained to grow into the best and most beautiful hedges. They obediently grow into whatever shape the gardener wants. At one time the whole of Europe was talking about the architectonic forms of the living yews in the pleasure gardens of Versailles. Topiary sculptures of animals of all kinds were sent out in special packaging to Russia and Sweden. Today this sort of 'trained' yew can be seen here and there in Scotland. They rarely allow themselves to be transplanted. Trees taken from a wood die when transplanted into gardens. Yews cannot bear too much light. In the open countryside they seek out the shadiest locations and lime-rich soil.

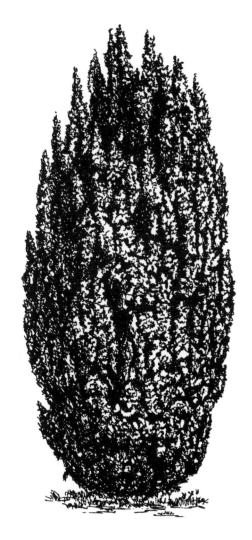

Unlike other conifers, the yew does not produce cones, but little red berries. The fleshy red coating is edible. It is very soft and tastes sweet. But the seed inside it is poisonous to warm-blooded creatures. The leaves, or rather the needles, can also be dangerous to horses, donkeys and cows, for example. On the other hand, deer and wild boar can eat twigs without coming to any harm.

Yew wood is the hardest and toughest of all the European trees. When it is green it is extraordinarily pliant and flexible. For this reason it was the preferred wood of bowmen. Dry yew wood possesses an exceptional weight-bearing capacity, which is needed for crutches and walking sticks, or the struts of larger umbrellas. Its high density and resistance to breaking make it suitable for hand implements such as clubs, maces, hammers and flails. But costly chests and other valuable items of furniture were also made from it.

Nowadays the furniture industry would love

to use yew wood. But it has become as rare as ivory and it takes far, far longer than any other tree for a yew sapling to become a fully-grown tree. A yew has to be 25 years old before it can set seed, and after that its growth slows down considerably.

Nobody can say with any degree of certainty just how long one would have to wait for this tree, which has its sights fixed on eternity, to achieve its full size and its optimum value. It takes at least a good two centuries-worth of patience. In England this requirement has already been assimilated as part of our heritage. For we already have world-famous yews in the churchyard in Bradbury in Kent, and age-old specimens in Eastwell Park near Ashon and in Crowhurst in Surrey. You will still be able to wonder at them there in a thousand years' time, for it is said that yews can live to be twice as old as oaks.

Originally the yew occupied the place which the fir now holds, from 2 to 11 January and from 5 to 14 July. There, with the hornbeam, it flanked the centre of the summer and winter solstices. Two indestructible hardwood trees therefore stood to the left and right as protection for the 'sweet' fruit trees, the fig and the apple, which themselves are direct neighbours of the beech and the birch.

The beech, as the symbol of law and necessity, must be permeated with love (the apple tree) and

creative strength, otherwise order becomes fos-
silised, the community becomes ossified and necessity turns into terror. The fig tree on the other side of
the beech symbolises the sweet reward which comes
to those who keep the necessary laws and the lawful
need. The beech, at the point of the winter solstice,
together with the apple and fig trees, is the symbol of
fatherly love, that is the love that is bound by conditions.

     The birch, which stands at the point of the
summer solstice opposite the beech in the tree circle,
symbolises, together with the apple and fig trees,
mother love, the unconditional love for which every
creature yearns. We have become acquainted with
the birch as the tree of initiation. But initiation into
what? On the one hand, initiation into the sweet fruit
of the Knowledge of Good and Evil (the fig tree), and
on the other hand, into the love that heals and unites
everything (the apple tree). Access to this 'trinity of
protection' of the birch, the apple and the fig is given
to mankind through the overcoming of death (the
yew) and reverence for life (the hornbeam).

     But the yew has another unspoken, secret
place, behind the walnut tree, during the days from
3 to 11 November. There it forms the anchor of the
'cross of uncertainty' made by the poplar. The days
of the poplar occur in spring from 1 to 14 May, in

summer from 5 to 13 August and in winter from 4 to 8 February. The poplar therefore comes 40 days before and 40 days after the oak. In summer it comes 40 days before the olive, and 40 days after that come the secret days of the yew. The 'cross of uncertainty' (the poplar) which intersects the circle, ends in the certainty of death (the yew) where it also has its roots. Thus the yew also has a right to three time periods during the year, since in its essence and its meaning it has a particularly dynamic effect on the dramatic play of life. But it forgoes these and leaves a large space for the walnut. The tree circle should be made up of three times seven trees, not 22.

Fir or yew? If we want to remain true to the Celtic spirit then we must clearly opt for the yew. We must renounce the fir. Only nothing new comes from this renunciation. Something old, which the Romans tried to eradicate, and which the Christian Church later persecuted even more, celebrates resurrection. But what is new is that it is not just any kind of authority that decides which tree should be given preference. I leave the choice above all to the readers who were born between 2 and 11 January and 5 and 14 July.

Gem stone: The white opal, which brings reconciliation with mortality.

Number: 0.

Medicinal use: In homeopathic doses, a preparation made from the needles of the yew stimulates liver function.

Motto: Death is something which gives weight to every moment.

FURTHER READING

Three main themes have run through this book: the trees, the Celts, and numbers and time. In a book of this size much detail has inevitably been omitted, and for those who would like to learn more about the individual themes, the books listed below are recommended.

TREES

Trees of Britain and Northern Europe by Alan Mitchell. Dragon's World: Limpsfield, 1985.

Blätter von Bäumen by Suzanne Fischer-Rizzi. Heinrich Hugendubel: Munich, 1994.

The Illustrated Encyclopaedia of Trees, Timbers and Forests of the World by H. Edlin and M. Nimmo. Corgi: London, 1981.

Ein Baum ist mehr als ein Baum by Frederic Vester. Kösel Verlag: Munich, 1986.

Bäume lügen nicht. Das keltisches Horoskop edited by

Annemarie Mütsch-Engel. Verlag Bert Schlender: Göttingen, 1985.

Meetings with Remarkable Trees by Thomas Pakenham. Weidenfeld & Nicolson: London, 1996.

THE CELTS

Celtic Mysteries: The Ancient Religion by John Sharkey. Thames & Hudson: London, 1975.

The Way of Wyrd, Tales of an Anglo-Saxon Sorcerer by Brian Bates. Arrow: London, 1986.

La femme celte by Jean Markale. Payot: Paris, 1984.

The Druids by Stuart Piggott. 2nd ed., Thames & Hudson: London, 1975.

The White Goddess by Robert Graves. Faber & Faber: London, 1961.

NUMBERS AND TIME

Of Time and Space and Other Things by Isaac Asimov. Dobson: London, 1967.

Time by Norbert Elias. Blackwell: Oxford, 1984.

Histoire universelle des chiffres by Georges Ifrah. Seghers: Paris, 1981.

Lexikon der keltischen Mythologie by Sylvia and Paul F. Botheroyd. 2nd ed., Eugen Diederichs Verlag: Munich, 1995.

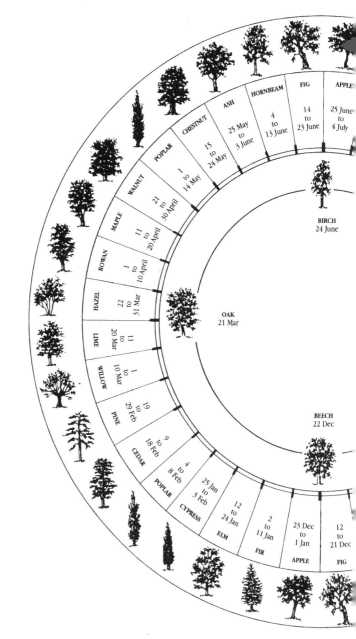

OAK
21 Mar

BIRCH
24 June

BEECH
22 Dec

POPLAR	1 to 14 May
WALNUT	21 to 30 April
MAPLE	11 to 20 April
ROWAN	1 to 10 April
HAZEL	22 to 31 Mar
LIME	11 to 20 Mar
WILLOW	1 to 10 Mar
PINE	19 to 29 Feb
CEDAR	9 to 18 Feb
POPLAR	4 to 8 Feb
CYPRESS	25 Jan to 3 Feb
ELM	12 to 24 Jan
FIR	2 to 11 Jan
APPLE	23 Dec to 1 Jan
FIG	12 to 21 Dec
CHESTNUT	15 to 24 May
ASH	25 May to 3 June
HORNBEAM	4 to 13 June
FIG	14 to 23 June
APPLE	25 June to 4 July